T0326598

# The Value of Voice in Shared Leadership and Organizational Behavior

# The Value of Voice in Shared Leadership and Organizational Behavior

Jamey M. Long and Joseph A. Pisani

ANTHEM PRESS

Anthem Press
An imprint of Wimbledon Publishing Company
*www.anthempress.com*
This edition first published in UK and USA 2023

by ANTHEM PRESS
75–76 Blackfriars Road, London SE1 8HA, UK
or PO Box 9779, London SW19 7ZG, UK
and
244 Madison Ave #116, New York, NY 10016, USA

Copyright © Jamey M. Long and Joseph A. Pisani 2023

The author asserts the moral right to be identified as the author of this work.

All rights reserved. Without limiting the rights under copyright reserved above, no part of this publication may be reproduced, stored or introduced into a retrieval system, or transmitted, in any form or by any means (electronic, mechanical, photocopying, recording or otherwise), without the prior written permission of both the copyright owner and the above publisher of this book.

*British Library Cataloguing-in-Publication Data*
A catalogue record for this book is available from the British Library.

*Library of Congress Control Number: 2022943266*
A catalog record for this book has been requested.

ISBN-13: 978-1-83998-520-1 (Hbk)
ISBN-10: 1-83998-520-8 (Hbk)

Cover image: Designed by Jamey M. Long and Joseph A. Pisani

This title is also available as an e-book.

The Value of Voice (VoV)

# CONTENTS

# PREFACE

There have been many books written about shared leadreship. What makes this book important in its field is that it furthers the leadership dynamic in developing the Value of Voice (VoV) as the connecting foundation to create a new and unified organizational culture. There is a change from "me" to "we." Decision-making is decentralized through stakeholder voice and valuing diverse perspectives and experiences that each member of the team brings to the process of meeting established goals. This book answers the question about how there is a breakdown between groups within a business or organization.

This book shares fundamental practices that any leadership team or organization can implement to address the knowledge gap created between stakeholder groups. Since most stakeholders have operated in separate environments, a silo effect has developed causing a devaluation of voice. Through some careful evaluation, behavioral organizations can capitalize on the diverse experiences of all stakeholders and use these experiences to develop more refined action plans.

Within the value of voice lies culture. Every organization is unique; therefore, each will have its own cultural norms. However, the same elements required to establish culture and voice will need to be applied. The elements of voice must begin with the development of a shared vision. The stakeholders will then identify the cultural values within the organization and shared mission. This situation is done through a systemic process that embraces inclusion and valuing voice. For voice to have a true (not just perceived) value, there must be engagement by each group of stakeholders so that the original "me" voice becomes the "we" voice.

The question becomes, how do leaders actively engage multiple internal and external stakeholders in a dynamic process of communication that values voice and engages all member within its structure? Every stakeholder should have a meaningful contribution to the continuous growth of the behavioral organization through sharing their lens as they work toward meeting the established expectations of the organizational goals. It is our goal that your leadership team will be able to implement these practices with our new model to help improve the VoV within your organization (i.e., small business, company, government agency, school).

# Chapter 1

# INTRODUCTION TO SHARED LEADERSHIP AND VOICE

Traditional leadership models have focused on developing the skills of the leaders and how they can better maximize their abilities to motivate and make informed decisions. The challenge with the traditional model is that many decisions made in isolation are made using inaccurate or incomplete information. Many times, the many stakeholders within a behavioral organization or school system do not share the information they know. The reasons for this lack of sharing are many; trust is a significant factor in the apprehension to share information. However, the most significant aspect for the lack of sharing of essential information is that the stakeholders do not believe they have a voice in the direction and path of the organization or school.

As a result, organizations and school systems tend to retreat to the "tried and true" status quo of prior actions and processes to address current issues. There was comfort and familiarity in the processes leaders had employed in the past, especially if their decisions have met with success. The truth of behavioral organizations and school systems is that they are ever-changing with expansion and contraction happening simultaneously. Therefore, it is improbable that a leader would have all the details and all relevant information when attempting to make decisions on current happenings. The decision process must change. How leaders engage their stakeholders, how they develop interactive and engaging processes for the sharing of information and how each member is valued for their understanding of the circumstances are critical for making the best choices possible. The collective and individual understanding is called their lens. The lens is how each stakeholder or group of stakeholders sees circumstances that are part of the behavioral organization or school system's environment.

The current reality in many organizations is that the three main groups are not effectively communicating and sharing essential information that will help support the growth and success of the operating systems. Behavior systems or how the organization functions are dependent on the collection and use of information to make operational decisions. Manager/leaders work

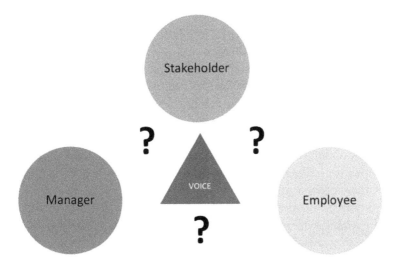

**Figure 1**  Silo leadership.

within a silo and do not capitalize on the knowledge and understanding of the other members of the organization. Unfortunately, in a traditional model these members also are operating within silos. They are not effectively sharing and working collaboratively for the success of the organization. When employees and stakeholders work in isolation and are not building collaborative processes, there is the likelihood that there will be redundancies in operating systems that also include inefficiencies that will impact the organization or school. The traditional system does not inherently value the collective voice. The traditional system in fact limits and stifles the voice and wisdom of the organizational groups.

A better process that has become more prevalent in behavioral organizations is to incorporate a leadership model that does value the collective voice. The shared wisdom of all members of a behavioral organization is to help develop better decision matrix and to enact better operational plans to ensure the success of the operating systems. In this model, there is a developed process where each of the members of the organization can share their lens and voice to help build capacity of understanding when faced with operational decisions. The managers/leaders can gather the perspectives from each of the groups and use this gained insight to better determine a path forward, essentially, making more informed decisions based on the vast majority of the shared understanding. To do this, the manager/leader must embrace a decision-making process that involves all groups within an organization and values the individual voice of each group member that will help make better decisions and ultimately ensure the growth and success of the organization.

Shared leadership occurs when two or more members engage in the leadership of the team in an effort to influence and direct fellow members to maximize team effectiveness (Bergan et al., 2012). The key aspect that powers shared leadership is that the members of the organization are working collaboratively to foster a process and develop decision outcomes that will shape the direction of an organization. The significance of this process is that members are serving as coleaders in the process. There is still a needed next step for how the voices of each member that is valued in the process of gathering and eventually making a decision. How each member's perspective is given value in the planning and implementing of the action steps is developed through the decision process.

It is important to distinguish shared leadership from team leadership because shared leadership describes how team members influence each other and share responsibility for tasks, rather than the concept of a team being led by a specific leader. Shared leadership occurs when a group of individuals lead each other to achieve successful outcomes (Carson et al., 2007).

Shared leadership has some essential structural components that must be within the organizational environment. Each of the stakeholders must have a belief in the shared mission of the organization, they must feel supported in the shared process and their voice must be valued. Without these three components, the attempt to implement shared leadership will most likely cause stakeholders to feel that they are not important and therefore their voice is not valued in the decision process. In developing a system for shared leadership, a manager/leader must foster an environment that actively engages the stakeholders. Having an understanding of the shared mission of the established shared goals, providing emotional support of each stakeholder and valuing the voice of each stakeholder as an important contributor to the process are essential building blocks the leader must develop within his operational system.

How the stakeholders understand the operational goals, the process that will be used to develop decisions and action steps and how the members stay focused to the established goals are critically important to the success of the organization. However, prior to this leadership process, the stakeholders should have the skills of shared leadership to work collectively to develop the shared goals. Are these goals important for the organization? Will developing these goals and eventually developing an action plan to implement changes based on the goals be agreed upon by the stakeholders? Without creating this shared vision of where the organization is moving toward, the work of the stakeholders will create a lack of clarity of process and outcomes. How the members share their support of one another is a component that often is overlooked in the drive to make decisions that create change. However, the endeavor to offer emotional and intellectual support of each member, valuing the contributions and voice of each is important to help keep the members motivated and engaged in the decision-making process. Feeling valued and having the recognition of the members of each person's contributions is how the members will build trust in each other and the decision-making process. Because of the trust created among each member, the process can build real value of voice for each stakeholder within the behavioral organization. By furthering the valuing of voice and the contributions and work of each member, there will be a dynamic developed by the members, and better decisions will be made to support the growth and success of the behavioral organization.

There is an importance in identifying your ideal work situation and taking steps to find or create it. The ideal work situation for an individual is to produce a desired amount of income so he or she is able to meet the basic physiological needs of food and shelter. Once those needs are met, an individual will need to generate additional income that will help to accommodate the desired lifestyle as well as save money for retirement in the future. While a job is used to provide a certain amount of income for the hours that are worked during the week, an ideal work situation will be required to increase the quality of life and satisfy all of the needs of an individual.

An ideal work situation will help an individual to become satisfied with the company they choose to be employed. When choosing a career and company to work for, it is important for an individual to study each factor of the position. While a job will bring money, it may not provide a high level of intrinsic or extrinsic rewards to the individual. This situation makes it important for an individual to consider the potential benefit of the position in order to gain satisfaction from the work being done. As a result, the individual will want to find a job that will satisfy the needs, wants, and caters to the strengths of their characteristics.

In order to create the ideal work situation, an individual will need to engage in "job crafting." Job crafting will benefit both the individual and the company. Since employees are a company's most valuable resource, the more involved the individual is in his or her work, the more will be his or her contribution to the overall productivity and therefore the morale of the organization. This situation will lead to a higher level of involvement and commitment by the individual that will benefit them on a personal level as well as improve the productivity of the organization. As a result, an individual will want to choose a company that will provide the freedom and flexibility that enables them to grow based on their personal characteristics and skill set.

Finally, an individual will need to understand their personal characteristics when choosing a job or an organization. The strengths and weaknesses of each person will be important since they will be used to satisfy the internal needs of the employee as well as the external needs of the organization. The goals and values of the individual must be consistent with the company. As a result, the individual must be able to provide an additional value to the company and to be able to gain personal satisfaction from completing the work and the needs of the position.

There are ethical risks involved in observation, as well as unobtrusive measures in job performance within a company or an organization. First, there could be a "fear factor" involved. Any perceived fear on behalf of the person being observed could alter the results. This could have both a positive and negative effect on the results of the data. Since the individual knows they are being observed, he or she will either perform at a higher or lower level than normal based on their perception of the observer. Another ethical risk with observation is consent, coercion, and concealment. This means that every individual should be made aware they are being observed. This is especially important when there are under-aged children, medical patients or when security issues can arise. The next ethical risk relates to the political motives behind the study. The data being collected may be conducted to support a wanted hypothesis and not for true research purposes. If the data are used to support a political motive that an individual does not currently believe in, it can cause an ethical dilemma. Finally, there is a potential ethical issue with observer training.

Finally, the results of the data could be flawed. If the data are manipulated to answer the "who, what, where, when, why and how," then the findings of the observer are misleading or false. This would break the good faith relationship between the observer and the individuals in the study. In the use of unobtrusive measures, ethical issues can also arise. Since researchers do not physically observe the participants, they must use other resources to gather the data. Resources that can be used are databases, databanks, journals, periodicals, digital media, and other technological resources.

Next, there is a difference between a mission statement and a strategic mission and both should be considered when establishing the value of voice within the organization or the company. The mission statement is used to explain three important concepts of the business. The first concept is who the company is; this is important because it specifically identifies the company's products or services to its customers and stakeholders. The second concept is what the company does; this is important because it states the customers and market segment that the company plans on serving. It also identifies the specific needs of the buyer and how the company will meet those needs with its products or services. The third concept is why the company is here. Each company is formed for specific reasons, and it is these reasons that give a company its identity. Since each company is unique, it is important to state the purpose of the company and reason it was founded.

The mission statement of a company is primarily used to communicate the current beliefs and values of the company. It is created by the top management team. It is the overall purpose of a company and helps to define the current objectives. The mission statement helps to identify the company's goals, and how they will achieve them. It also defines the main objectives that need to be met in order to satisfy the needs of the customers. The mission statement is also focused specifically on the present and not the future. The intended audience of a mission statement is its internal customers that include employees, managers, leaders and stakeholders. Finally, a mission statement should always incorporate and reference the company's core values and strategic vision so the needs of the customer can be achieved.

Unlike the mission statement, the strategic vision is focused on the future. It is concerned about where the company is going. The strategic vision focuses primarily with the future course of the company and communicates this direction to all internal and external customers that include government, employees, managers, leaders and stakeholders. Such a vision must be communicated to both top management and also to the regular employees. If every employee does not understand the strategic vision, the company will be unable to act as a cohesive unit. Without a clear vision, there will be a strong resistance to change. This lack of action will cause the company to become stagnant and not grow.

The strategic vision helps the company to define where it wants to ultimately go in the future. It also communicates the unique values and purposes of the company. A good strategic vision will help to inspire and motivate the company's employees so they will maintain a high level of productivity. It is important that the vision be descriptive to help set and reach achievable results. This helps to express the company's desire for a hopeful future with realistic results. The strategic vision also helps to align the company's culture with its values in order to bring everyone together to work as a single team. It is important to make sure that company's mission statement and strategic vision are linked together. Together, they help to express the core values and beliefs so that it clearly defines a well-defined roadmap for both the present and the future of the company.

To better understand the value of voice, we must first define the terminology that is most commonly used throughout businesses, companies and other organizations.

## SWOT

A SWOT analysis is used to analyze a company's strengths, weaknesses, opportunities, and threats. The SWOT helps to determine the company's overall situation. The main question the SWOT analysis answers is if the company is in good competitive standing. Good competitive standing is necessary for a company to be successful in pursuing new and attractive market opportunities while being able to maintain a competitive advantage against external threats. The SWOT analysis looks at both the internal and external factors of a company. The strengths and weaknesses are internal and look at what the company is currently doing well. The opportunities and threats are external forces that could either benefit or harm the company. A SWOT analysis is significant because it will help a company to understand its internal and external environments.

## Core Competence

A core competence is an internal activity that is "central" to a company's strategy. A core competence centers on what ability a company is most proficient at and does best. The core competency is what allows the business to have competitive advantage and is a valuable strength and asset to the company. It can be a business process, model, product or pricing structure.

Companies that have a core competence want to make sure to leverage its usefulness in order to guide its business processes. A core competence can also help a company to introduce new products or market segments and increase its competitive advantage in their industry.

## Distinctive Competence

A distinctive competence is a task or an activity that a company performs better than any of its competitors in the industry. A distinctive competence is more valuable to a company than a core competence. A distinctive competence is not just the ability a company performs at a high level, but it also is a distinct advantage that its competitors do not possess. Finally, a distinctive competence ensures that a company can sustain any changes in the market while offering an unrivaled product to its market segment.

## Stakeholder

A stakeholder is an individual who has an investment within an organization. The investment of the stakeholder can be direct or indirect. The stakeholders of a company will give the direction of the company. The primary goal of a stakeholder is to earn a profit from their investment in a company. The profit earned by a stakeholder is determined by the success of the company and its ability to use organizational resources to effectively achieve objective and goals. While a stakeholder is not an employee, they are considered a member of the company.

## Value Chain

A company value chain is a collection of the business activities that gives the business and consumer value. In order to provide value to a customer, a company needs to be able to produce a reliable product or service. Each of the processes needed to produce the product help to add value. The value chain looks at both the primary and supporting activities of the business operation. The departments that are included in the value chain are the supply chain management, operations, distribution, sales and marketing, services and the company's profit margin. Together, each of these departments work together to add to the overall value of the company and the products or services that it offers its customers.

With these terms, we are now able to understand and define the competition and potential within business industries. There are five forces that underlie the five forces model of competition. The first factor is the threat of new entrants. When the industry environment is profitable, existing businesses will experience an increase in competition from outside firms that want to increase their financial earnings. The new entrants into the market will steal market share from the existing companies. This situation will result in a loss of revenue and profit for the companies and their shareholders. Finally, the threat of new entrants will force existing companies to develop a new strategic management process to compete more efficiently and effectively in the market.

The second force is the bargaining power of suppliers. The more power the suppliers have in a particular market, the more they control the pricing and cost for the organization. Supplies have the ability to increase the price while decreasing the level of quality that is sold to a company. As a result, organizations are forced to absorb the cost and reduce its amount of profit or to pass the cost on to the customer through increased prices. The third force that underlies the five forces model of competition is the power of buyers. If the economy is good and there is a wide product selection for consumers, the purchasing power becomes controlled by the consumer instead of the firms in the industry. This would make it difficult to set prices or to predict a steady return on investment or to generate above-average returns. Finally, the bargaining power of buyers will enable the consumer to dictate the price of outputs causing the business strategies to change to a low-price cost structure which will lead to reduced returns for investors.

The fourth force is the threat of substitute products. Substitute products will impact competition by promoting new products into the existing market segment. This situation will cause the firms to lose their competitive advantage since they will no longer have a proprietary product to offer consumers. As a result, consumers will be able to control the pricing of prestige products since they have the option of buying a similar product from another party. This situation will cause financial instability in the market and the inability for company to maintain long-term sustainability.

The final force that underlies the five forces model of competition is the intensity of rivalry among competitors. When an industry has a low level of competition, the firms that operate in the market are able to control and dictate the price of a product. The companies will also experience long-term growth and above-average returns for their investors. However, industries with intense rivalry will lose the ability to generate a profit based on the competitive actions of the other firms. When a company challenges the existence of another firm in the market, the initial firm must spend additional resources to compete to maintain its market share. This situation prevents a firm from generating a profit and to expand in the industry analysis. As a result, the higher intensity among competitors will reduce the ability of smaller companies to remain in existence in the industry.

A cost leadership strategy can allow a firm to earn above-average returns in spite of strong competitive forces. A cost leadership strategy is used to help a firm gain a competitive advantage over the other competitors in the product market. When a firm uses a cost leadership strategy, it seeks to devise and implement the lowest cost point required to conduct its business processes to produce and sell outputs. The ability of a firm to successfully utilize a cost leadership strategy depends on its level of efficiency, scale, scope and size. As a result, a cost leadership strategy is gained through economies of scale and scope the by knowledge, skills and abilities a company learns by competing in the market segment.

Social responsibility applies to all businesses that operate in the goods and service sectors. This strategy does not only apply to large-scale corporations but to small businesses as well. The social responsibility of a business will help to build long-lasting relationships with consumers in the market segment. It will also help to improve the quality of life by implementing a business strategy designed to support consumers and the environment in the long-term development of the economy.

Based on previous perceptions, social responsibility was mainly thought to be managed by large corporations. However, the majority of businesses in today's global economy are small companies. The small businesses include sole proprietors, partnerships and limited liability companies. To compete with large corporations, small businesses must rely on social responsibility to strengthen their relationships with consumers in the market. Social responsibility has become a strategic component for small businesses to provide additional value to consumers by giving back to the community it serves.

In the past, social responsibility was thought to only apply to organizations whose stakeholders were philanthropic and had a desire to influence the wealth and knowledge of other people. Today, social responsibility is necessary to help organizations to become transparent and to adopt an internal culture that supports the needs of the environment. This situation will enable a company to improve its knowledge base and to become more involved in the market segment. The company will have a high level of quality and values that will gain support of the employees and consumers. As a result, the company will experience an increased level in profit and long-term return on investment.

Next, social responsibility will allow a company to improve its brand name image and consumer loyalty. When a company is able to demonstrate its ability to benefit its customers, the consumers will pay a premium for its goods or services. Social responsibility will lead to the objective and goal achievement. Companies will experience a higher level of involvement and commitment from consumers, employees and the local government based on its commitment to protecting the market. Social responsibility is also important to minimizing the level of risk for an organization. The more conscientious a company becomes of the different variables within a market segment, the more a company will be able to develop a strategic plan to eliminate new entrants and to provide consumers with high-quality goods and services.

Finally, social responsibility is required in order for a company to remain loyal to its shareholders. The main purpose or goal of a business is to provide its stakeholders with a high level of profit and return on investment. Every action of a company should be conducted with the thought of the shareholders. This situation will cause both large and small businesses to be aware of the needs of the shareholders and to remain responsible. To maximize the wealth of the stakeholders, a company will need to gain the support, trust and loyalty of the consumers to increase profits and market share. As a result, the wealth of shareholders will increase and the consumer market will experience an improvement in the environment and quality of life.

Social responsibility is consistent with the current attitudes and beliefs about business. In today's economy, companies must implement social responsibility into their strategic plan to adopt their focus and achieve objectives and goals. For social responsibility to succeed, each organization must take ownership of its actions and perform in an ethical manner that benefits the entire market. Next, social responsibility must become an important driving force for today's top managers and small business owners. This strategy will enable a company to establish a corporate culture based on ethics and the inclusion of the consumers in the market.

As a result, the company will be able to grow and expand in the market based on its dedication and support of improving the quality of life. Large corporations will continue to remain in existence. Small businesses will be able to expand and grow into new markets gaining economies of scale and scope. Finally, social responsibility will provide companies with a stronger brand name image. Consumer loyalty will continue to expand based on the amount of effort and resources the company contributed to adding actual and perceived value to the lives of consumers and shareholders in the economy.

Next, we must understand stakeholders, and who they are. There is the difference between primary and secondary stakeholders. It is very important for companies to make this distinction. Primary stakeholders are made up of different groups. The first group is employees. Employees are stakeholders because they are an organization's most valuable resource. Employees will perform at a high level for the organization when they are rewarded for their effort and dedication. Next, investors and shareholders are primary stakeholders. Investors and shareholders provide the organization with financial resources and security to operate in the market.

Customers are also considered primary stakeholders. Customers include internal and external individuals who interact with the organization. The consumers are the end-users of the outputs produced by the company and dictate the demand of the outputs. The needs of the customers will help guide the direction of the company. Finally, communities and governments are primary stakeholders. Communities and governments will provide a reliable infrastructure for the company. This situation will help to develop the rules, policies, and expectations of the market environment.

There are several different types of secondary stakeholders. The first secondary stakeholder is the media. The media is a secondary stakeholder because it is not directly tied to the company. However, the media has the ability to promote the organization to the consumer markets. Organizations will want to collaborate with the different media venues in order to gain positive publicity for their goods and services in order to gain a competitive advantage. Next, trade associations are secondary stakeholders. Trade associates assist in the development and sales of an organization's outputs. A company will want to form a strong relationship with trade associations in order to become a dominant force in the market and industry. Finally, special-interest groups are considered secondary stakeholders. Special-interest groups assist organizations by supporting the rights of the different groups or members of employees. This situation enables a company to provide added value and support to its workers in order to gain employee loyalty and to improve efficiency of the business process.

Now Cultural Intelligence (CQ) and the Leader-Member Exchange (LMX) theory must be understood. CQ is the movement of ideas across various cultures and economic markets. In today's global environment, the traditions, values and customs have been moved and transferred from one area to another. This situation has resulted in the shared ideas and beliefs that have created a singular culture. As a result, the consumers and communities of the world have the ability to share in a common or shared experience. Organizations are also able to benefit from CQ in order to meet the needs of both internal and external consumers through the diversity and a better understanding of the needs of a global society.

There are three main components to cultural intelligence that include cognitive, motivational, and behavioral. Cognitive involves the knowledge and understanding of the different system in the global market. In each market segment, there are different economic, legal, ethical and social systems. This situation enables a company to understand the different subcultures in each market segment or divisions within the community it operates. Second, cultural intelligence is motivational. Motivation occurs internally to each individual and internally or externally to an organization. Motivation provides an individual with the ability or desire to learn about other cultures. The more motivated an individual becomes, the more focused he or she will become in fully understanding different motives and paradigms. Next, motivation leads to the full understanding of a situation. Individuals who are open to learning the importance of subcultures are able to address current and potential issues in an efficient and effective manner.

The final component of cultural intelligence is behavioral. The behavioral component is required to provide individuals with the ability to improve communication. Different cultures use verbal and nonverbal skills differently. This situation makes it important for organizations and top managers to understand the difference in verbal cues in order to avoid any negative perceptions. Failure to understand the background and proper mode of communication or behavior will cause a company to be perceived as not caring about the different subcultures of the communities around the world. Finally, the more effective a company is involving each employee in understanding the different cultures and backgrounds in the world, the more cultural intelligence the company will gain. As a result, the company will gain market share, additional profits for shareholders, and also become more ethical and socially responsible in each of its actions.

One of the most extensive elaborations of leadership as a relationship is found in the LMX theory. Leaders within an organization develop and form a unique and individual relationship between each follower. Over time, the LMX creates a different relationship and exchange between the leader and the follower. A small number of people that follow a leader are called the "in-group," while the majority of the followers form an "out-group." The "exchange" process between the leader and the different work groups evolves based on the quality of relationship and level of trust.

The LMX theory analyzes two concepts between the leader and the followers. The first is investment. Investment is determined by the amount one party gives to another party. When a leader provides a high level of time and resources into their followers, the investment level is high. If the group of followers does not support the leader, there will be very little investment, and there will not be a beneficial member exchange. The second concept is based on the level of return. Return is based on what one party receives from another based on the exchange process. If a leader is able to gain the belief and support of his/her followers, there will be a high level of return, support and productivity.

However, if the leader is ineffective in developing a reliable exchange membership, the amount of return will not exceed the level of investment. As a result, there will be a poor level of results and quality management. The stronger the "exchange" process is between the leader and his/her followers, the greater the return on investment. The essence of the perspective on the leader–member relationship is the LMX theory linkage or relationship between the leader and the different group members. Each relationship is different and will have its own value or merit for both parties. The relationship is "dyadic," meaning it is a special relationship based on the investment and return of two people. The "in-group" of followers will be given more opportunity and responsibility because of the structure of the membership exchange. The exchange between the leader and the group members is not random. The level of exchange is based on the personality and perception of value between the leader and the follower.

As a result, the LMX will impact the quality of management within an organization. The greater the exchange, the higher level of motivation and inclusion the follower will have in the work environment. This strategy will enable the leader and employee to form a relationship that benefits both parties and will have a higher rate of return. Leaders will invest more time and resources in employees that they believe will ultimately perform at a higher level. Leaders will want to establish as many high-quality relationships with as many followers as possible. This situation will enable the leader to have a larger "in-group" and a small "out-group" that will lead to an increase in quality and productivity.

There are several steps to the development of the leader–member relationship. First, leaders must meet with each employee in order to establish the nature of their specific relationship. Second, the relationship exchange that is the most promising between the leader and followers will become the "in-group." The rest of the members will become part of the "out-group" with less trust and responsibility. Next, the relationship between the leader and members of the "in-group" will grow and expand over time, creating a greater commitment to the success of the organization's mission and vision. The leader will reward the most valuable "in-group" members for their level of exchange and commitment. Finally, the LMX depends on constant communication and follow-up in order to increase the amount of return of the exchange process.

Organizational justice and its impact on the LMX must always be considered as sensible and fair. This strategy will enable the organization to maintain a strong relationship between the leader and the different work groups during the exchange process. Next, it is important for leaders to provide an "in-group" LMX process to every employee. Once the "in-group" work experience has been provided, the leader and follower will be able to better define their relationship over time. This situation will determine the expectations and results of the relationship and will also utilize a high level of organizational justice. However, followers who are in the "out-group" through the LMX will be judged based on their performance and will be evaluated and will receive a specific role based on distributed justice.

The implementation and perception of organizational justice must be maintained during the LMX process. A transfer from a partial lens to a complete lens will form between "individual" departments to an all-inclusive organizational perspective. What will drive this process in change is the reward and disciplinary actions within the company or the organization. Rewards or disciplinary actions cannot be given to employees without a valid reason or explanation for the course of action. Failure to implement organizational justice will cause the LMX process to decline and will be replaced by a large "out-group" and smaller "in-group" of workers. The success of organizational justice in the LMX must recognize and incorporate procedural, distributive and interactional forms of justice. This strategy will enable the organization to build strong long-term exchange relationships between the leader and each worker.

The LMX process is dependent upon trust. Trust is defined by the values and perceived expectations between two individuals. Trust has different inherent behaviors that include ethics, honesty, respect, responsibility, virtue, integrity, justice, fairness, loyalty and honoring promises. It is determined and established by the character and exchange between two individuals. The ability and confidence to rely on another individual, based on a level of respect, are important to accomplishing objectives and goals. Trust is also an important factor in forming a strong LMX within an organization.

Trust is most important in the actions of the leader and their actions in all past and current experiences. The trust between the leader and the follower will determine the perception and success of the outcome of a situation. Trust is also necessary to establish transactional and transformational leadership. Transactional leadership focuses on formal authority and defined roles of individuals within an organizational setting. This form of leadership will enable the leader to manage employees based on a series of fair rewards and discipline based on individual actions. Transformational leadership requires a leader to gain trust from their followers to identify the need for change and to inspire a new vision to implement the necessary change.

Trust is important in establishing participative decision-making. Trust will also influence the follower's ability and desire to believe in the leader and organization. The length and term of the LMX will determine the level of trust. As a result, there will be a unique relationship between the leader and the follower that will promote care and concern for the welfare of both parties. Finally, trust is important in establishing a positive work environment and increasing job performance and satisfaction.

Next, the trustworthiness of a leader is directly linked to the member's job performance and commitment to the objectives and goals of the organization. Third, trust will guide procedural, distributive and interactional forms of justice. The trust in a leader is based on the attitudes and behavior and their relationship to job performance. Finally, trust is important in the LMX because it allows for everyone to be involved in the decision-making process. As a result, a consensus can be determined by the entire group, and everyone is responsible for the outcome of the situation.

Nearly two decades after the publication of the Stogdill review, Edwin Locke and several of his graduate students took another look at the trait literature. Kirkpatrick and Locke stated that traits appear to endow an individual with the "right stuff" to be an effective leader, yet traits are merely important preconditions. Kirkpatrick and Locke believed that traits were important "preconditions" that provided an individual with the potential to be a successful leader. An individual who becomes an effective leader is not necessarily chosen because of their intellectual knowledge. However, the individual becomes a leader based on their ability to be a "great man" or "great woman" that was either born or made.

While an individual must be endowed with the "right stuff," the traits of a leader are only an indicator of establishing potential leadership. Leadership is a difficult and unyielding position with an enormous amount of responsibility. As a result, leaders cannot be an ordinary person with generic characteristics or traits. However, having the right traits is only part of being an effective leader. An individual will not experience leadership until he or she is in the right place and time where their traits are needed to handle a particular situation. The location of the situation is an important factor to leadership since it provides the physical structure or reason for leadership.

However, it is the knowledge and ability of the individual to manage and control the variables of the situation. Only a person with the "right stuff" can properly handle the various opportunities and challenges of the situation. Leaders must use their traits to show their charisma in order to gain control of a situation and influence the "in-group" in order to be successful with the desired goal or objective.

Kirkpatrick and Locke proved that along with preconditioned traits, there were four keys to successful leadership. First, the motives and traits of the leader must be accepted and coincide with the present situation in order to influence a group of followers and develop a large "in-group." Second, effective leadership must include the use of knowledge, skills and abilities, which will determine the number of followers and the success of the overall goal. If the leader is unable to convince a group of his or her abilities, the leader will lose confidence, and the goal will not be achieved.

The third key to successful leadership is vision. Leaders must have a unique and clearly defined vision. A vision is important to persuading a group to follow the leader's strategic plan. A leader that is able to communicate and get the buy-in from the followers will be able to form a large "in-group" that will work toward accomplishing the stated goal. The final key to successful leadership is the implementation of the vision, which is the final stage from changing an idea into a reality. The leader must use their knowledge, skills and abilities to find the right way to make the desired change and to achieve the overall goal. Together, these four strategic components will form the essence of effective leadership.

Leadership power is the most complex form of power for a leader. It is determined by a job or position within an organization and forms legitimate power. An individual that holds a particular position within an organization will be given power or status based on the needs of the organizational structure. Each individual is given some form of legitimate power in order to work together to achieve a common goal, mission or vision. The legitimacy of power is not always based on the requirements of an organizational role. It can be determined by the values of an individual and his or her commitment to a personal code, ethics or acceptable standard. Legitimate power is influenced by the culture of an individual. Culture can provide a framework for the legitimacy of power and shape which individuals are expected to hold a higher level of control through leadership positions. Legitimate power will occur based on the perception and acceptance of the authority of the leader within the social structure and culture of the organization.

Finally, legitimate power defines the power of a position within an organization as well as the characteristics and traits of a specific individual. As a result, legitimate power will be determined by the perception of the individual's legitimacy or motives. If the leader's decision-making and actions are made for the right reasons, the level of legitimate power will increase. However, if the leader misuses their power for personal gain, the group will lose confidence, and the level of legitimate power will decrease based on the individual's actions.

The leadership structure of P-12 schools causes some unique challenges in developing a culture of shared leadership. The major stakeholders within a school setting have defined roles that are structured to allow for autonomy of action and decision-making. Teachers work in their classrooms engaging with students and creating learning opportunities for students. These learning opportunities are within a learning environment that is based on the development and creation of relationships between the teacher and the students. This shared environment is led by the interactions between the teacher and the students.

The relationship between the teachers and the leadership team is another version of the same structure that confines interactions and the exchange of ideas and perceptions. The teachers have a long-standing belief that the school leadership is disconnected from the dynamic interactions that happen every day in the classroom. The leadership team believes that their understanding of a more global perspective of the mission and the vision of the school. This disconnected dynamic has caused a culture crisis in schools. It is through the active engagement of all stakeholders and developing structures that allow for the authentic valuing of a variety of voice.

It is the valuing of voice that presents the most challenges for leaders to overcome. How can leaders work to develop a culture of shared leadership that embraces and engages stakeholders' voice is the most important task to develop a culture of inclusion and growth? It is this work and the steps that both leaders and stakeholders can take to work toward the real development of a shared leadership model and a school culture that embraces the value of voice. It is through this system that schools can then begin the work of creating a mission and vision that will be reflective of all stakeholders and is a shared understanding of what is essential for the success of the school and all students, teachers and staff.

If leaders are not open to the perceptions and vision lens of all stakeholders, and they use their leadership power without valuing the voice of all stakeholders, then the school culture will be toxic and not support the endeavors of the teachers and the students. How the leader behaves as a leader has more impact on how the culture within the school will develop than any other

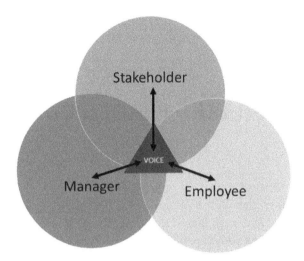

**Figure 2**   The synergy of shared leadership.

member of the school community. The school will be reflective of how the leader behaves and how the leader interacts with the other stakeholders. It is incumbent upon the leader to not only model shared leadership practices but to also genuinely believe that the ideals of shared leadership will help to make the school a better organization that is reflective of the collective beliefs of all stakeholders.

As the concepts of shared leadership and the process of valuing voice that will be further developed in this book, it will help both leaders and all stakeholders to better understand their roles with the learning organization. How to better address the challenges and concerns of the stakeholders and how they can work together to create a more collaborative and a more reflective environment of the shared beliefs of all stakeholders is a critical part to the success of the synergy of leadership. That the mission and vision developed through the collective actions of all stakeholders will reflect the essential core values that all share as part of a community of learners.

## References

Bergan, J. Z., Rentsch, J. R., Small, E. E., & Davenport, S. W. (2012, Jan-Feb). The shared leadership process in decision-making teams. *The Journal of Social Psychology*, *152*(1), 17–42. https://doi: 10.1080/00224545.2010.538763. PMID: 22308759.

Carson, J. B., Tesluk, P. E., & Marrone, J. A. (2007). Shared leadership in teams: An investigation of antecedent conditions and performance. *Academy of Management Journal*, *50*(5), 1217–1234. https://doi.org/10.2307/20159921

# Chapter 2

# SHARED LEADERSHIP

Deciding to develop a shared leadership methodology, the organization must decide if the members will support this change in leadership ideology. Interventions to encourage shared leadership are most effective when organizations are utilizing teams to achieve organizational objectives (Carson et al., 2007). Organizations can utilize shared leadership principles within teams, either with a designated formal leader or in teams without a designated leader (Carson et al., 2007). Vertical leadership does not need to be discarded and shared leadership can improve the internal processes within a team (Carson et al., 2007). One of the misconceptions of shared leadership is that the organizational structures and hierarchy must be dismantled for the shared process to work. This is not accurate; the leadership structures that have been implemented in the organization can remain, and how the leaders activate the other stakeholders in decision and leading process.

To overcome the established leadership structures, the stakeholders must be within an environment that has clarity of role and clarity of goals. The stakeholders must have comfort in the organizational environment and know that they can have strong supports from the other members. There must be a clarity of goals and how meeting these organizational goals will benefit them and the organization. When developing a shared leadership model that values voice of all stakeholders, it is important to have the operational organizational environment of inclusion and shared importance developed and implemented first. Without having this type of operational environment established prior to empowering the stakeholders, there will be role and responsibility conflict and the process of shared leadership will breakdown and fail.

There has been prior research that has established the importance and value of shared leadership and developing effective teams. This research also established that the use of shared leadership improved organizational performance. The influence of implementing effective shared leadership is more impactful on stakeholder actions than an engaging charismatic leader. Shared leadership has the greatest impact on stakeholder effectiveness and productivity than any other leadership style or organizational system. Overall, shared leadership showed the strongest relationship to team effectiveness (Wang et al., 2014). By developing strong shared leadership systems, organizations will have stronger collaborative stakeholder behaviors and great belief in the value of each member involved in the decision-making endeavor. The power of shared leadership is evident in the gathering of varied perspectives and knowledge. The stakeholders have unique skills and lens to each dynamic of a decision-making process and the ability of the leaders to harness these skills and lens will determine the impact of the developed outcomes.

The role of the leader has tremendous impact on the operation of the stakeholders and the dynamic of the team that has been charged with the decision-making tasks. Leaders need to embrace a role of support and facilitation. The leader must understand that they set the tone and tenor of the interactions of the stakeholders. If the leader is driven by authority and controlling thought, the shared leadership process will fail because stakeholders are not feeling valued and do not trust the intentions of the leader. However, if the leader assumes the role of being an active listener and facilitator of the stakeholders, the members of the team will feel that their voice is being valued as being essential to the overall process and eventual final outcomes. Leaders need to have confidence in their abilities as leaders as they assume secondary roles during the interactions of the stakeholders.

Leader personality is also important in supporting the development of a shared leadership process. The leader needs to demonstrate a model of being honest in their abilities and skills. Honor the limitations of skills and areas of need as a leader. Being open with the stakeholders about what areas of strengths and weakness are within the leader will help each member of the team to see their place within the group. This will allow stakeholders to fill these areas of need and assume the leader role for that aspect of the team endeavors. Each stakeholder will identify their areas of strength and how they can support the leader in helping to refine the dynamic of the group's work. Stakeholder ownership of the process, leading specific aspects of the group's work and sharing perspective and wisdom will ensure that the group will embrace the challenges of decision-making and being agents of change for the organization.

There are some challenges to using shared leadership and valuing voice. The decision-making process that incorporates shared leadership takes time. Significantly more time than autocratic decision-making. The interactions of the stakeholders and the development of consensus take time. There are times within a behavioral organization when decisions must be made quickly to address crisis. When addressing systemic change and operational shifts in the behavior of the organization, it is far better to encapsulate the decision within the interactive dynamics of shared leadership. Additionally, trust is important to have honest discussions among the stakeholders. When the trust is violated, and there are actions either by the leader or other stakeholders that diminish the voice of others, the process will break down and fail.

The ineffectiveness and challenges to trust can be addressed by the leader as they begin the shared leadership process and engage the stakeholders. The beginning of the shared leadership process allows the leader and the team to create the systemic foundations of the team. How the team will function, how each member will be valued, and the varied perspectives will be incorporated in the development discussions can ensure a more successful team endeavor. The development of team norms and operational behaviors that help guide the work and interactions of each stakeholder will help to keep the team focused on the established goals and outcomes. When addressing challenges to shared leadership processes, it is important to be cognizant of the role each stakeholder will have on the team. How has the construction of team addressed diversity of experiences, perspectives and beliefs? For the process to work best, it is important for varied lens to be shared during the discussion and development of decisions. It is through these varied lenses that the team gains greater insight and learns to trust and value the voices of each stakeholder.

The leader along with the stakeholders must begin by developing a shared team vision. The development of the vision is how the collective goals and work of the team are maintained to ensure that the team remains focused on their collective outcomes. Once the vision and goals are established and agreed upon, the leader must create opportunities for stakeholders to act on the behalf of the team. To act in the best interests of the team stakeholders must believe that they will be supported as they challenge the status quo and move to become agents of change. Stakeholders are taking risks to be part of the shared leadership process and leaders need to support the stakeholders, but it is also important that the stakeholders support the leader during this time of change. The challenge of change is that some members of an organization might be resistant to change and may act to undermine to movement toward new goals and procedures. All stakeholders must feel that they are being supported to take risks and work toward the decisions needed to implement change.

Once the stakeholders feel that they can be trusted and are being supported, they can collectively work toward developing an action plan for change. They can feel that there is a collective responsibility and ownership in the decision-making process as well as the action plan that will be implemented to support the change. To accomplish this, stakeholders need to believe that they can question the status quo, that they can question why certain processes are in place and why certain systems are in operation. Through the questioning and challenging of the past practices, the stakeholders can develop a more focused and refined action plan. How does the organization's environment sustain the shared leadership team and allow for follow-through of decisions that will impact system success? Is there a climate within the behavior organization that supports the stakeholders and trusts the decisions and action plans developed by the team? If so, then the process of shared leadership has been successful. If there is doubt, then the process will not yield the results anticipated by the organization.

Rules will need to be established for shared leadership to occur. One type of rulemaking is hybrid rulemaking. Hybrid rulemaking involves the formal and informal creation of policies and procedures within a business that forms the foundation of rules and culture. It is a mixture of both formal and informal agency rulemaking. Hybrid rulemaking was developed as a solution to the problems administrative agencies faced when regularly making rules that were in agreement with the established procedures. In some states, hybrid rulemaking is required by law. Next, hybrid rulemaking is used in multistate

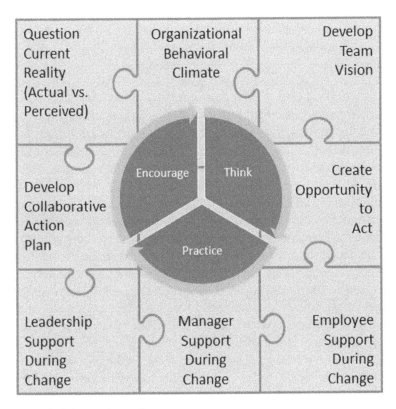

**Figure 3**  Think, practice and encourage.

rulemaking. Rules that require different levels and stages to be completed will require a combination of both formal and informal rulemaking. Third, hybrid rulemaking is necessary in the creation of an informal record. Finally, hybrid rulemaking is used in the issuance of detailed reasons and findings within a case.

There is a big danger in crafting a competitive strategy for managers that are torn between the pros and cons of the various generic strategies and opting for a "stuck in the middle" strategy that represent compromises between lower costs and greater differentiation and between broad and narrow market appeal. In today's global market and changing economy, it can become difficult to know what the right strategy is to use at any particular time. However, managers should avoid a "stuck in the middle" approach. While it might seem like safe strategy, in the long term it will hurt the company's competitive advantage and cause it to lose market share. When choosing a strategy, managers must remember to develop it around the core values and competencies of the company. This strategy will ensure that the manager is best utilizing the company's resources and positioning itself firmly in the market that it operates.

Strategies for competition include low-cost, broad differentiation, focused low-cost, focused differentiation or best-cost. Each of these strategies is designed to give a company a distinct advantage over its competitors. In order for the strategy to be effective, a manager must make sure to commit to that specific strategy and focus around the company's operations and strategic vision. Each of these five strategies will position the company differently in the market environment in which it competes. The core strategy that is chosen will be the main driving factor to determine how the company operates and how successful it will become in the market against its rivals.

Finally, managers that implement a "stuck in the middle" strategy will not be able to determine if they are serving a broad or narrow market segment. In order to serve a broad market segment, companies will want to focus on producing large quantities of items and a lower cost. For a narrow market segment, companies will focus more on product differentiation and there will be higher costs associated with each product that is made given the lower economies of scale in its specific niche. If a manager does not structure the strategy around the strategic vision, the results will cause the company to have average sales revenue and become stuck in the middle of the industrial pack and will never become an industry leader. Companies with a "stuck in the middle" competitive strategy will be seen as average to the consumer causing the consumer to choose its rivals as a better alternative for products and services.

There is a great deal of value to the firm when it has a specified vision and mission. A well-conceived strategic vision helps prepare a company for the future. A well-conceived strategic vision is also important to help make sure that company and its stakeholders are focusing all efforts of the company in a single and unified direction. With today's changing economic conditions, it is important for companies to have a defined strategy to help them in the future. If there is no strategic plan, there is not strategy for the company to follow. This would cause a breakdown in communication and organizational structure and design.

The mission statement of a company is primarily used to communicate the current beliefs and values of the company. It is created by the top management team. It is the overall purpose of a company and helps to define the current objectives. The mission statement helps to identify the company's goals and how they will achieve them. It also defines the main objectives that need to be met in order to satisfy the needs of the customers. The mission statement is also focused specifically on the present and not the future. The intended audience of a mission statement is its internal customers that include employees, managers, leaders and stakeholders. Finally, a mission statement should always incorporate and reference the company's core values and strategic vision so the needs of the customer can be achieved.

Assessing the value of a mission and vision, organizations can capitalize on a value chain analysis process. Value chain analysis tracks and follows the output from the initial raw-material stage to the final sale or transfer of ownership to the consumer. The main goal of value chain analysis is to provide a company the ability to generate as much additional value as possible to the strategic management process. The value creation will need to be created as cheaply and affordably as possible in order to reduce the cost of the output for the consumer. Next, the value chain analysis is necessary for managers to be able to identify and analyze all of the individual activities in the manufacturing process.

Managers will be able to determine which processes or components will maintain or create additional value for the consumer. As a result, the more value a company can generate through the value chain analysis, the greater impact the output will have on the end user. Finally, a value chain analysis should be used to determine all of the strengths and opportunities of competitors in the same market or industry. There are two main types of activities that are included in the value chain that include the value chain activities and support functions. Value chain activities are all of the activities that a company must complete in order to manufacture or produce outputs.

Once the outputs have been produced, the company is able to sell, distribute and service. This strategy enables the company to create additional value for consumers. The next type of activity is the support function. The support functions are all of the various activities or tasks the organization must complete in order to support the primary activities being accomplished through the value chain activities. When an organization has used its core competencies to complete value chain activities that competitors are unable to duplicate, then the firm has created a new competitive advantage. As a result, the company will be able use the value chain to create strategic competitiveness in the global market.

Managers are motivated to diversify based on value-reducing reasons when focusing on the mission and vision of the organization. Value-reducing diversification is utilized by top managers to reduce their personal level of risk of unemployment and decreased financial return on investment. Top managers can use value-reducing diversification only as long as their actions do not impact the overall profitability of the company. As a result, value-reducing diversification will vary based on the individual motives of the upper managers within a firm.

The primary reason that managers are motivated to diversify is to increase the level of job security for senior executives within a firm. When an organization experiences a high level of diversification, the level of risk of the manager is decreased. If a business unit fails within an organization, the senior manager will lose their position within that division. However, the use of value-reducing diversification will enable the manager to maintain employment in another division or business unit within the company. As a result, the manager is guaranteed continued employment and has a low level of personal risk associated with the success of the business division.

The next managerial motive for diversification is that it will increase the size and stability of the organization. Diversification will increase the size of the firm by expanding into new industries and product markets. This situation will lead to an increase in executive compensation. As a result, diversification will lead to the creation of improved compensation plans for the top managers that include pay package designs, equity compensation, vesting and performance-contingent pay.

Finally, managers support diversification within a firm based on the increased profit and reward structure. When a firm diversifies, there is an increase in the amount of work and responsibility. This situation increases the need and value of the upper managers within the firm. Diversification will provide the ability for managers to earn higher salaries and compensation for their work performance. As a result, managers are motivated to diversify for individual and selfish reasons. However, the more selfish the reason of the senior manager, the greater the reduction in the amount of compensation and profit a firm will create for its shareholders and investors.

There is also an effect of the separation of ownership and control in the modern corporation. The control ownership and control of an organization is controlled by the mechanisms established by the senior managers through corporate governance. Corporate governance is used by companies in order to implement policies and procedures to control the business environment. Companies that implement a high level of corporate governance will experience more control over the daily business processes. This situation will enable a company to use official methods of checks and balances to monitor employee performance and to improve the effectiveness and efficiency of the production of outputs. As a result, the company will experience a tighter alignment within its culture and organizational structure in order to improve the decision-making and actions of the firm. Corporate governance helps identify and determine the organizational rights and responsibilities among different individuals within a company that include the board of directors, top management, employees, consumers, stakeholders and shareholders.

Next, corporate governance will improve or change the nature of executive and managerial decision-making by establishing a high level of accountability. Accountability is critical within an organization because it will focus and guide the decisions of each executive to support the vision and strategy of the company. Corporate governance and alignment will provide and determine a strategic business strategy for the entire company. This strategy will ensure that every managerial decision and action made by an executive will be based on the need of the entire organization. The company will experience decision-making that supports the culture and structure of the firm.

Finally, corporate governance will improve or change the nature of executive and managerial decision-making by providing minimizing the level of risk. Companies that rely on corporate governance will be able to perform internal audits. Internal audits will be used to analyze every business decision or action by an executive to guarantee that the company is following the best course of action. Auditing will also enable a company to control each decision of an executive through monitoring the impact of each action. This strategy will allow a company to provide oversight and become involved in every step of the decision-making process before any action is taken. As a result, the company is able to become more socially responsible to it market segment, reduce risk and maximize profits for its shareholders.

Under governance, there are three major types of organizational structures. Organizational structure is very important for a firm in order to gain a competitive advantage. The main purpose of defining the organizational structure is to describe the "formal" and "informal" actions within a company. Formal organizational structure will establish the rules, regulations and hierarchy within the firm. An informal organizational structure will determine the social and culture configuration of an organization. Firms will need to determine the appropriate organizational structure base on the goods and services it provides to consumers in the markets.

The first organizational structure is a simple structure. Companies that implement a simple structure are typically small. The owner or manager is responsible for making all of the important strategic decisions for the company. Next, the owner or manager monitors and controls all of the activities that occur within the firm. Simple structure firms rely on informal relationships between the individuals performing the job duties. There are few rules that must be followed within the firm. Third, a simple structure will lead to a limited task specialization for the employees. Fourth, a simple structure will suffer from a lack of technology and innovation. The company will rely on using old equipment and limited resources that will prevent future growth. As a result, a simple structure will only work for companies that offer a single business unit or product line in a specific market. Companies can use a business-level strategy without having to have a strategic-level strategy to compete in the market.

The second type of organizational structure is a functional structure. A functional structure is important to organizations that utilize horizontal differentiation. Large organizations must group responsibilities into certain functions so different tasks can be completed simultaneously, decreasing the output time. As organizations grow and differentiate, there are several problems that can arise with a functional structure. Finally, strategic problems will occur when an organization grows and differentiates with a functional structure. The larger an organization becomes, new operational problems will arise. Managers will be forced to spend more of their time dealing with the day-to-day business operations instead of focusing on the future growth or direction of the organization. As a result, managers will focus on the short-term instead of the long-term goals. This situation will lead to a decrease in growth and profit for the organization. Finally, the organization will experience communication and integration problems. The managers in the different functions will become focused on their own division and not coordinate with the other managers. The organization will lose its focus and fail to remain a strong competitor in the business market.

The final type of organizational structure is a multidivisional structure. A multidivisional structure provides support functions and places them in self-contained divisions within organization. With the self-contained support functions, each division is able to control its own value chain and output process. This strategy allows the organization to become more decentralized at the top level but remain centralized at the functional level, increasing product quality and minimizing costs.

The multidivisional structure also uses the corporate headquarters staff that uses managers to direct the activities of the various divisions. The corporate managers add an additional level to the hierarchy of the organization. As a result, there is an increase in quality and control through the use of vertical integration. Finally, a multidivisional structure allows an organization to operate in several different business markets at the same time while a product division structure focuses on a single business unit. This strategy leads to increased organizational effectiveness, increased control, growth in profitability and a higher developed internal labor market.

Internal innovation occurs within an organization. In order to develop new products, a firm will use its R&D department to create new products or to develop innovative new features of its existing outputs. This strategy relies on the company's ability to use its human capital and new advancements in technology to create a new idea or product that can generate above-average returns in the product market. Next, internal innovation will enable a company to gain a competitive and comparative advantage in the market segment. As a result, the company will be able to increase its level of competition by strengthening its core competencies and value chain activities.

Autonomous strategic behavior and induced strategic behavior can be compared and contrasted. This behavior is part of the internal venturing process. Product champions will pursue new ideas through a political process. The political process required to pursue new ideas will enable the product champions to coordinate and commercialize the new output. This strategy will allow the firm to support the growth of the new idea until it is able to gain a strong position in the product market segment.

Induced strategic behavior is a top-down approach that enables a firm to use its current strategy when pursuing new ideas. The firm's current strategy will help to establish a structure and framework that will be used to facilitate and guide the process of new products and any innovations that correspond with the output. Before a new a strategy is developed to support product innovation, it is filtered through the various levels of hierarchy within the organization to ensure that it is consistent with the goals and objectives of the firm.

There is a high level of importance of human, social and relational capital in the workplace. Human, social and relational capital helps to strengthen the ability of an organization to increase its ability to negotiate in the workplace. First, human capital involves the labor workforce within the economy or workplace. Next, human capital includes the unique and proprietary skills gained by an individual through training, education and development. The more skills and knowledge an individual possess, the greater resource he or she becomes to the company. When an individual continues to gain knowledge through training and development, he or she is able to become more marketable based on the new skills they have acquired.

Next, an employee is able to gain a greater understanding of the work environment within the company. As a result, the employee will become more desirable since they will have a "big picture" understanding and be able to help in the negotiation process for the company. An example of human capital is a manager who seeks to gain an MBA or PhD/DBA in business. Gaining an advanced degree will help to increase the knowledge and understanding of the current manager which will gain them a higher salary and in turn benefit the company with the increased knowledge and understanding.

The second form of capital is social capital. Social capital involves the collective sum of the resources and individual has based on the result of their venture into social networks. The level of social involvement will help provide an individual with a competitive advantage in the hierarchy of organization. This situation will result in individuals with a higher level of social capital moving quickly up the "corporate ladder" based on their direct involvement in specific social networks. Social capital provides a critical resource for developing a strong consumer base in order to improve business. Social capital also helps to strengthen the negotiation process since it relies on the pre-established relationships with the individuals involved in the conflict resolution.

An example of social capital would include lawyers, consultants or small business owners. Lawyers, consultants or small business owners would need to rely on their social capital to strengthen their customer base. In order to gain business, each of these individuals would need to maintain a positive relationship and be viewed as desirable by the customers. Failure to form strong relationships with the consumer would cause the lawyers, consultants or small business owners to lose business to other employers that have a higher level of social capital.

The final type of capital is relational capital. Relational capital is a form of social capital that is primarily used in negotiations. Relational capital analyzes the dyadic relationship that develops during the negotiation process and the accrued relational assets. Next, relational capital will increase based on the individual's commitment to strengthening the level of trust, commitment and partnership with the second party during the negotiation process. As a result, the improved relationship will lead to a more integrative form of negotiation strategy that will ultimately produce a successful resolution to conflict. An example of relational capital is a manager of a facility who has formed a strong relationship with each of the trade technicians that service their location. Finally, human, social and relational capital is combined in order to determine the current and future needs of an organization so it can improve its leverage when negotiating in the workplace.

Capital owned by a business creates power. Power often accrues to individuals who are very effective in their jobs or to firms that enjoy sustained high performance. Since this is true, power is different from basis competence, efficiency and performance. Next, power refers to the firm's ability to accomplish its goals by using its capital and other resources to form a relationship with a third party. The purpose of the relationship is to influence the third party to provide the firm with the desired inputs without a contract or an official agreement. The more power a firm accumulates, the more it will be able to control the suppliers, distributors and consumers in the market.

There are four sources of power that include legitimate, reward, coercive and resource dependence. The first type of power is legitimate. Legitimate power is a form of formal power. Formal power is given by the nature of the position within the business. The second source of power is reward power. Reward power is used by upper management to influence the behavior of employees through a system of incentives. The third form of power is coercive. Coercive power occurs when a manager relies on threats and negative consequences in order to comply with the directive of the firm. The final source of power is resource dependence. Resource dependence occurs when a primary principal reduces the reliance of other agent while increasing the agent's dependency on the primary principal.

Individuals who are very effective in their jobs or to firms that enjoy sustained high performance and accrue power within a firm. The power of an individual and their position will increase the more indispensable the employee becomes to the firm. If the individual must be replaced, the replacement for the individual will inherit the power of the position based on the success of the previous employee. This situation occurs due to the low level of substitution within the firm. The amount of power is determined by the strength of the firm compared to the external environment. Employees that perform at a high level in a competitive economy will gain power within a firm. However, when the economy is nonaggressive, then employees will not need to worry about being replaced. As a result, workers will remain complacent without fear of losing their jobs due to the power of the outside environment.

Finally, power is different from basic competence, efficiency and performance. Basic competence, efficiency and performance are focused on a commitment or contract to complete an objective or a goal. Power results from a lack of contractual agreement. The relationship between the principal and agent develops from other necessities instead of through a formal contract or expectation. As a result, power will dictate and control the behavior of the principal and agent regardless of a contractual agreement. This situation occurs when the success or best interest of one firm depends on the informal relationship with another organization. The culture and power of an individual are controlled by the structure of the internal and external environment of the market.

It is possible to identify the powerful people within your organization. Powerful people within an organization can be determined using certain indicators. The first indicator of a powerful person within your organization is the control of organizational resources. Assets are critical to the development of outputs. Individuals who control the resources of an organization will determine the course of the firm. If another manager wants to use the resources of a firm, they will need to make a logical argument and convince the person in charge of the resources that it is the best course of action.

The second indicator used to identify the powerful person within your organization is formal power. The person who possesses a formal title within an organization also has the power associated with it. The third indicator is the individual within the firm who is considered the "go to" person. The "go to" person is the individual who everyone within the firm will seek out to solve the problems or to combat the weaknesses or threats of the environment.

Smircich and Morgan (1982) provide us with insight into leadership by focusing, in part, upon what it is that leaders do. Smircich and Morgan suggest that leaders "frame reality" and "manage meaning" for followers. There is a perceived right by certain people to choose and define the reality of the situation. This paradigm will determine the needs of the individuals in the situation and the necessary perception of leadership that is required.

In an unstructured environment, leadership will naturally emerge due to the shared needs and understandings of the group. It is the expectations of the other members in the group that will choose an individual and to implement their style of leadership. The role of the leader and the leadership process is formed out of the interaction between the leader and the followers during a particular action. The group is willing to delegate power to the necessary individual in order to manage a situation. This strategy allows the leader along with the group to define the perception and reality of the situation which will guide the course of action. As a result, leadership is created by creating a "point of reference" and a clear path to follow.

A leader's "frame reality" occurs when the events in a situation of an event cannot be controlled. However, the context or the setting of the situation that is experienced can be defined or labeled. It is the leader's responsibility to effectively communicate the framework of the situation in order to provide the proper type of leadership and to guide the followers through the event. Once the context and situation are defined, the leader must apply the right ethics and guidelines for the situation in order to establish the proper context.

Fourth, the "frame reality" must interpret the uncertainty of the situation. Leaders are required to interpret the level of uncertainty and contingency plans to get to lead the followers through the ambiguity of the event. Fifth, the "frame reality" will design the response to the situation. It is important for leaders to understand the problem so they can design a solution for the particular context in order to persuade the followers. Finally, it is necessary for leaders in the "frame reality" to communicate and affirm their chosen course of action in order to assure the followers that the right decision has been made.

Smircich and Morgan also suggest that "manage meaning" is necessary for followers. "Managing meaning" focuses on the way that the meaning of an action or a situation is interpreted or perceived within society. Leadership is the foundation of a conventional paradigm or belief system. There is an important relationship between the leadership figure and the ground structure. The actions of leadership influence and define the meaning of context. While the leader guides the action based on their experience, the importance of the action is assumed and interpreted to engage the action. The final action is then based on the thought process of the leader. This situation causes a management of meaning for a certain event or action. Based on the dependency of the action, the role of leadership is formalized and institutionalized.

Leadership and management are required in the leadership process and the LMX. Leadership is a process that influences individuals to achieve a stated goal or objective. The main components of leadership are that it is process oriented. Second, leadership uses influence to convince individuals to complete a task. Third, leadership requires a follower that is directly involved in the context of the situation. Finally, leadership involves achieving a stated objective or goal.

Management is the execution of a task or process. Management, or headship, is the supervisory and administrative functions that are used to oversee the process. Headship is critical to the directing of activities and controlling the individuals that are involved in a situation in order to achieve the stated objective. Management is based on an infrastructure that utilizes personnel and available resources. While leadership focuses on the influence and motivation of individuals, management focuses on the completion of the work and is based on results.

Leadership and management (headship) share many similarities. First, leadership and management use influence to motivate people. Second, both tactics involve working with people and groups. Third, both strategies are used to work toward achieving a specific objective or goal. When managers are working toward a specific goal, they are utilizing leadership to influence the people involved in the process. When leaders rely on planning, organizing and implementing a process, they are using management to accomplish the goals.

However, leadership and management also have several differences and distinctions. The role of the leader of an organization is to inspire and guide the employees. It is essential for the leader to motivate each employee and to make them involved in achieving the goal or objective. Second, leadership involves the development of ideas while management focuses on creating and maintaining the process. Third, leaders inspire trust and creativity, while management focuses on performance measures and control. Fourth, leadership has long-term goals, while management focuses on ensuring results in the short term. Finally, leaders are innovative and encourage originality, while management imitates and implements trusted business processes to properly analyze the results of a situation. Leaders lead people, while managers manage situations.

Leadership involves an individual that directs followers to achieve a specific goal or task. There are two types of leadership. This first type of leadership is formal. Formal leadership comprises the power and authority given to an individual by the organization. Formal leadership is determined by the written rules and documentation provided by the organization that states the level of authority and power of a specific individual. The goals, duties and expectations of formal leadership are clearly defined by their title or position within the organization.

The second type of leadership is informal. Informal leadership does not have an assigned figurehead or official leader. Instead, informal leadership occurs when a group of people elect an individual to guide them during an action or event. An informal leader is chosen by the group which believes that a certain individual is the best person to provide guidance and motivation. When the dynamics of the situation change, the group can elect a new informal leader to guide them. Informal leadership arises when there are shared goals and objectives by a group of people. The informal leader is chosen based on his/her individual experience in a given situation. Informal leadership is not an official position within an organization and has no defined authority.

There are several differences between formal and informal leadership. First, formal leadership is used in an established organization. The rules and expectations of the leader are defined by the position and authority of the organization. With formal leadership, employees seek the approval of the leader. Each employee is given a certain amount of power in the organization. The power and authority of the individual are static and do not change based on different situations.

Next, formal leadership involves specific rights and privileges to support an authoritarian title defined by an organization. However, informal leadership is not determined by any level of official authority. Third, formal leadership has the ability to issue discipline and punishment for wrong behavior. Formal leadership can also issue compensation and rewards for performance, while informal leaders cannot. Finally, informal leadership is achieved by utilizing successful means of communication and individual personal relationships. Formal leadership relies on policies and is enforced by the structure of the organization. While a formal leader can lead by a position of authority, an informal leader must lead by example.

There is a process through which individuals with a certain set of traits might emerge in leadership roles. First, traits are an important part of the leadership process. In some cases, it is believed that "great men" and "great women" are born with the necessary traits to be a leader. These chosen individuals are believed to possess certain characteristics and traits that enable them to become an effective leader. The first common trait of leadership traits includes intelligence and the capacity to learn. Next, leaders will have the ability to achieve in order to accomplish objectives and goals. Third, leaders will be dependable and will inspire responsibility. Fourth, leaders will be highly adaptable to situations and will encourage participation with the group or individual follower. Finally, leaders will have a high level of popularity and acceptance. The status level of the authority and position of the leader will give him or her a prominent position within the environment.

Next, the process through which individuals with a certain set of traits might emerge in leadership roles is based on the nature of the leader. Individuals in leadership roles can either be proactive or passive in nature. A proactive leader looks for a situation that needs leadership and addresses the need for change. A passive leader has developed traits that cause that person to not interfere with a problem until it becomes severe and can no longer be ignored. In order for an individual to emerge in a leadership role, their personal traits must match the needs of the situation so there can be a successful exchange process.

While certain characteristics and genetically conditioned traits are an important precursor to leadership, experience is not related to the performance of a leader. Having the knowledge to solve a problem does not provide the right opportunity or situation to convince other people to follow a particular direction. A leader is able to utilize a beneficial exchange process and use people and resources to work together to solve an objective or goal. While an individual may possess the understanding of a problem, leaders have a trait that enables them to coordinate a group activity and create a large "in-group" to accomplish the goal.

Finally, a successful leader emerges based on their traits and ability to effectively influence the different parts of the leadership process. First, leaders must be able to communicate their motives and traits to the group of followers. Next, leaders will use their traits to demonstrate their knowledge, skills and abilities to improve performance. Third, the traits of a leader are necessary to communicate a shared vision. The traits of a leader are used to inspire confidence so the necessary course of action can be implemented to achieve their vision.

According to Conger (1990), the dark side of leadership is the visionary leader. While visionary leaders may have pure intentions, there is the possibility of their actions to produce negative results or outcome. The dark side of leadership occurs when the leader has a failed vision. First, leadership is based on the vision and perceptions of the leader. As a result, the dark side of leadership will occur when the vision is based on the leader's internal needs instead of the support and success of the group followers.

Second, the miscalculation of resources required by the leader will impact the success of the vision. Third, the dark side of leadership will cause the leader to have unrealistic expectations and distorted goals for the market segment. This situation will cause the leader to make decisions and to take actions based on wrong information. As a result, the leader will waste valuable resource and time, causing the group to experience failure and a breakdown in the leader-member exchange process. Fourth, leadership's negative face will cause visionary leaders to not recognize the changes in the environment. This failure will lead to the leader's inability to redirect their vision to meet the actual needs of the new environment instead of focusing on the perceived requirements.

There are several forces that give rise to the dark side of leadership. First, visionary leaders who make their personal needs paramount will produce a negative outcome within the organization. Leaders who only focus on personal needs and success will fail to produce positive results for the group of followers or the organization. Next, leaders who become like a pyrrhic victor who believes that victory must be obtained at any cost. Third, leaders who chase a vision before its time or before the resources are available will cause a negative impact on the organization.

Fourth, visionary leaders can come to deny flaws in their vision. As a result, leaders will perceive that their actions are producing negative results but will continue to pursue the same course of action in order to avoid admitting failure in the decision-making process. Fifth, visionary leaders will use manipulation in order to create a perceived impression with the group of followers. This strategy will enable the leader to gain the support and trust of the followers based on false data instead of the truth of the situation.

Sixth, visionary leaders will communicate and manage upward and sideways. This situation will cause the leader to distance him- or herself from potential supporters and to cause conflict within the organization. As a result, the manager/leader focuses on "being special" and is perceived as selfish instead of a supporter within the organization. The dark side of leadership will cause a breakdown in LMX. Leaders will become overbearing and will override any thought process or decision-making ability of the followers that contradicts his or her vision. Finally, visionary leaders will implement informal management and bypass the formal level of authority. This situation will lead to a breakdown in the chain of command and will also fail in providing support to the group of followers in the organization.

When dealing with people, leaders want to make sure to not succumb to Machiavellianism during the LMX process. Machiavellianism is a general strategy for dealing with people. Leaders who utilize Machiavellianism believe in the philosophy of using duplicity and deception as part of the LMX process. Machiavellian leaders believe that people will perform actions by being manipulated into certain situations or events. These types of leaders implement tactics that will manipulate and misguide the group members in order to support the self-serving purpose of his or her vision. The different Machiavellian tactics that leaders use are deception, cunning and expediency in order to demand immediate action on behalf of the followers without giving them time to process the consequences of the decision-making process.

There are several dangers associated with leaders who have a strong Machiavellian orientation. First, Machiavellianism will have a negative impact on organizations when leaders only want to experience personal gain instead of focusing on supporting the success of the group. This situation will cause a leader to view their followers as an expendable resource. As a result, there will be a breakdown in trust, and the LMX process will fail within the current situation. The leader will sacrifice any organizational resource in order to gain personal success and to satisfy their own self-interest.

Next, Machiavellianism will lead to a leader's inability to look inside a problem and take responsibility for his or her own actions. Next, mirroring will occur under Machiavellianism leadership. Mirroring will be implemented by the leader to force individuals to view the leader the same way the leader perceives him- or herself.

Third, Machiavellianism leadership will cause an individual to become narcissistic. Narcissism generates a false or distorted view of their actions and intentions, including a high level of intolerance of criticism and the inability to recognize any fault in the decision-making process. Next, emotional literacy will develop as a result of Machiavellianism leadership. Leaders with emotional illiteracy are unable to verbalize their emotions for the greater good because of their misperception and self-serving interests.

Finally, Machiavellian leaders will develop unwillingness to let go. The Machiavellian leader's actions become dysfunctional and no longer meet the demands and expectations of the job. However, leaders that have a Machiavellian orientation are unable to accept any responsibility or blame for the dysfunction within an organization. Instead, these leaders blame the group members and the variables within the environment for the failure of not achieving their vision. Machiavellian orientation will cause the leader to become self-destructive and will also cause learned helplessness with the other group members in the leader-exchange process.

Within companies and organizations, conflict will naturally develop due to the competition for resources and power. There are certain conditions that can cause conflict to be good or bad for an organization. In order to compete in today's global economy, organizations must grow and adapt to the changing and complex environment. However, organizations must also continue to meet the needs of each of their different groups of stakeholders. This situation can cause conflict to arise within an organization as the interests of the different groups compete for the same valuable resources. The higher the level of positive organizational conflict, the greater potential there is to become more effective within the business environment.

However, conflict within an organization may be perceived as positive or negative under the right conditions. Conflict can be good or beneficial to an organization in order to overcome inertia. Organizations that have become inert and are no longer active in developing new products or services will fail to compete with other companies. As a result, the organization will lose market share and its competitive advantage. Top management will evaluate organizational conflict and learn from its mistakes in order to make continuous improvements and practice total quality management. Since there are different viewpoints between top management and the stakeholders, organizational conflict will improve the decision-making process and enable the organization to better utilize its valuable resources.

Organizational conflict can also be negative for an organization. Organizations that are unable to come to an agreement and to properly allocate resources will experience a decline in productivity and revenue. Without a formal agreement or guidance toward a singular direction, the organization will continue to waste time and resources while competitors gain market share. When an organization wastes valuable time arguing or trying to bargain over issues, the hierarchy of the organization breaks down, leaving the company exposed to weaknesses and threats.

There would be a higher level of conflict in an organization with a mechanistic structure. With a tall organizational structure, the organization will have many levels of bureaucracy. When this situation occurs, it becomes easier for organizations to lose control at various levels within the tall structure. When there is a loss of control in a mechanistic structure, a high level of conflict will occur. While managers will have the ability to make decisions, they will also experience a lack of authority and will need to wait to proceed until the proper level of authority gives them permission. This situation will cause a delay in decision-making and for the organization to experience inertia throughout the hierarchy.

With an organic organization, there is a flatter hierarchy. This strategy gives lower-level managers and employees the ability to make decisions and determine the necessary course of action. An organic structure promotes cross-functional teams, and there is a mutual understanding between every employee to cooperate in order to complete the task. The proprieties and goals of the employees within an organic structure are shared, and there is no latent or outright conflict of scarce resources to cause the organization to become inert in its decision-making or business activities.

The creation of a shared leadership methodology is reliant upon the structures and systems that have been put into place by the leaders of the organization and/or school. Leadership type plays a significant role in developing shared leadership. If leaders believe they lead because of rationale-legal authority, or lead through a philosophy of intimidation and fear, the work they do to develop a shared leadership practice will fail. The failure is the by-product of the conflict of actions and statements. A leader cannot say they believe in shared leadership and then act in a manner that does not follow the essential tenants of shared leadership. Shared leadership embraces the dissenting voice. It is the challenges offered by stakeholders that question the purpose and process of changes to the culture. The voice that questions if the decisions being made are going to have the impact that the leaders believe it will have been an important part of the reflective shared leadership that will make the leader, the school and the stakeholders better.

How leaders engage and work with stakeholders who have a different lens of perception on a specific topic or action step will be one of the most telling endeavors of how skillful they are at being leaders. To build consensus among a team of stakeholders and have agreement of mission and vision many times feels like an impossible task. It seems every time the team moves one step forward, they have a disagreement and take two steps back. However, it can be argued that this very moment of disagreement and the subsequent conversations that the leader encourages are the very moments that the tenants of shared leadership is being enacted for the betterment of the organization.

Leaders need to lead the conversations that engage all stakeholders. They need to publicly celebrate the voice that disagrees with the vision, mission, and action steps. Leaders have to set the environment that allows all stakeholders to feel that there is a community of trust and that they have the opportunity to share their perspectives without fear of reprisal or criticism. Leaders are required to model this environment of trust. Even when the stakeholders do not follow the same actions of trust, the leader must enact the practice of trust. It is because of this trust that the environment of shared leadership and the valuing of voice will have a positive impact on the decision-making process and action planning of the team.

Schools have a unique challenge in developing a culture of trust because there are many environmental behaviors that by their nature are actions that erode trust. The process of evaluation and observation that is part of the school culture is perceived by the teachers as an adversarial endeavor. The us-versus-them or the me-versus-you mentality. In a shared leadership environment, that values voice can build a collective understanding of this very evaluation process and reduce the conflict and mistrust that has historically been a part of this contractual process. If the leader and stakeholders collectively work together to build a real understanding of the purpose of observation and evaluation, and how this is a process focused on growth then they can reduce the negative connotation that has plagued schools. Once this collective understanding has been developed through a shared leadership process, the leaders must honor the trust and the process they agreed too.

The better shared leaders use the collective process to open discussions with stakeholders about concerns and issues that are important to helping the school operate better. There are leadership responsibilities that must be accomplished by the leaders. There are operational obligations as well as instructional obligations. If the leader shared the expectations and the desired outcomes that are being required, then collectively the leader and stakeholders can work toward understanding the system and expectations, as well as understanding each stakeholders' responsibilities. The process must be open to different stakeholder voices. The more stakeholder voice is valued, and the leaders use shared leadership, the more the school culture will be reflective of the beliefs of the stakeholders. The path to improvement will be through the use of shared leadership and valuing stakeholder voice.

## References

Carson, J. B., Tesluk, P. E., & Marrone, J. A. (2007). Shared leadership in teams: An investigation of antecedent conditions and performance. *Academy of Management Journal, 50*(5), 1217–1234. https://doi.org/10.2307/20159921

Wang, D., Waldman, D., & Zhang, A. (2014, March). A meta-analysis of shared leadership and team effectiveness. *Journal of Applied Psychology, 99*(2), 181–198.

# Chapter 3

# IMPORTANCE OF VOICE

The importance of voice in the shared leadership process is the building blocks to the value of voice in a behavioral organization. It is important that each stakeholder feels that the organization supports their work and values their contributions to the process of decision-making in the organization. There is a need to begin by developing a collective understanding within the organization of the shared leadership process, its value to the organization and the responsibilities and expectations of each member of the organization. Without developing this foundation, the stakeholders engaging in shared leadership will not have the support needed to remain focused on the determined goals. The culture of the organization must be developed to understand and embrace the importance of voice. The climate within the organization must be one that supports the value of voice and embraces the varied lens each stakeholder has regarding the operation and function of the behavior organization.

Once the organization has developed a climate and culture that supports and values voice, then the stakeholders can begin to build consensus of voice. The process of developing consensus of voice will require each stakeholder to embrace and value the opinions and perceptions of each member of the organization. The stakeholders must become comfortable with a system where a wide variety of perceptions are shared from a variety of experiences. Role and experiences within the organization color the lens of each stakeholder. How each stakeholder receives information and shares their understanding of circumstance will help to develop a consensus of voice. Developing a single mission and vision for action and development of goals that will lead to action plans for change is important in implementing systemic improvement of the organization.

Creating an environment where voices are valued is only part of the process. Developing a system within the organizational environment where voices are now activated to help develop change is essential to sustaining shared leadership. Stakeholder voice shared within the team dynamic, activating the thinking and perspectives of others will ensure that there is a variety of thought and richer more refined action steps are implemented. It is this type of environment that activates voice, puts voice into action and helps organizations to be more proactive in their decision-making versus reactive to conditions that impact growth and success. An organization's environment must value voice, and it must embrace the variety of voice from the myriad of stakeholders that operate within its systems. The authentic valuing of voice will ensure that there is greater focus on the goals, and the action plans developed will address the needs of the organization. True valuing of voice is not about addressing the needs of the leadership, but of addressing the needs of the organization even if it is not the preference of the leaders.

Honesty and transparency in the process of valuing voice allow all stakeholders to share in a collective understanding of conditions relevant to reaching the established goals and having the same degree of information as the leader to better engage in the decision-making process. In valuing voice, the leaders must recognize the contributions of the stakeholders, there must be a way to compensate the stakeholders for their efforts. The process of compensation is not physical alone but can be the celebration and recognition of the efforts and value of each stakeholder. How their contributions have been essential to the success of the organization and how they helped to develop the action plans that will help to reach the agreed-upon goals.

The real value of voice is not just in the variety of perspectives that a shared leadership process offers but also the ability to tap into the expertise and skill sets of the stakeholders involved in the decision-making process. As organizations and schools react to continuous shifting demands and the need to continue to refine systems and processes; the ability to engage a variety of stakeholders becomes even more important. To engage stakeholders with a variety of experiences and with a wide range of skills, the process of improving operations will ensure to address organizational concerns. The challenge is how to engage and activate each stakeholder to capitalize on their skills and experiences. The leader must embark on a concerted effort to build connections and relationships between themselves and the stakeholders and eventually among the stakeholders. It is through this development of connected relationships that the importance of voice becomes an important part of the decision-making shared leadership process. As the team develops and further connects through these relationships, the stakeholders must agree to accept various points of view and varying perspectives. It is through the acceptance of the variety of perspectives and perceptions from the stakeholders that as a team the importance of voice drives decisions and solutions.

If the stakeholders recognize the importance of voice, then they also have to recognize the importance of the dissenting voice—the voice that disagrees with the process and/or action plan, the voice that questions the purposefulness of the endeavor and the voice that does not trust the process. The importance of voice is to hear all variations of stakeholder's perceptions and perspectives. To limit voice, to try and shape input from stakeholders or to refuse to allow free expression from the members of the team defeats the purpose of engaging in shared leadership. It reduces the value of voice as well as the importance of sharing voice. The strength of shared leadership is an unfailing belief in the importance of voice, even when it is uncomfortable to hear and address. It is through the difficult work of addressing the dissenting voice that the real value of the team's work gives rise to better decision-making and better planned action steps. Dissenting voice is equally as important as the agreeable voice. In many cases, the dissenting voice is even more valuable. The dissenting voice forces the stakeholders to think and reflect differently, to process information and to seek solutions differently. The importance of voice allows stakeholders to strive for success in meeting their agreed-upon goals.

Training and developing the value of voice and the skills to share voice are important first steps in building a culture that supports stakeholder's engagement and perspectives. The idea of valuing voice is not inherent in every person; it is a learned skill that is perfected over time. Stakeholders will engage in three main areas of professional development: building voice, creating trust and becoming active listeners. In truth, these same skills are essential traits of successful leaders. Building voice professional development will offer stakeholders skills in having the confidence to share their experiences and expertise with the team.

Creating the process for professional development in building voice should begin by giving stakeholders practice in sharing their experiences in noncontroversial events. Using a model of community circles with developed interaction norms with discussion prompts that are participant friendly is essential to help build the skills of sharing voice. Prompts that offer opportunities for participants to share their experiences while listening to the experiences of others also create opportunity for stakeholder to be reflective in their exchanges with members of the team. It is through the active sharing of voice and then listening with empathy and understanding that creates the conditions of valuing voice and gives the participants the practice in building their voice.

Creating trust within the group dynamic is a process of sharing voice, valuing voice and demonstrating understanding without judgment. Understanding does not mean that the listener agrees with the perspective; it means that the listener has demonstrated value in that this is their teammate's perspective. The listener then must honor the process of sharing and demonstrating to the stakeholder who shared their voice, the respect to treat them with humility and support. How listeners engage with the stakeholder who is sharing builds the foundations of trust within the group relationships. If the leader wants the stakeholders to work as a connected team, then there must be a culture of trust that has been developed over repeated interactions and time. How the leader and each stakeholder models trust and respect in the team dynamic will be the determinant if the group can function effectively and efficiently.

The skills of being active listeners is not just giving space for others to speak and listening. It is the process of internalizing what has been shared, offering value to the speaker and being accepting of varied perspectives. Active listeners use probing and reflective questioning to allow the speaker additional opportunities to share details and conditions to their perspectives. The professional development should offer participants the opportunity to practice these skills is a safe learning environment. One of the most difficult skills is to be an effective active listener. One that can engage the speaker and give space for sharing of ideas and beliefs. If the stakeholders can become skillful at being active listeners, the entire team will function with incredible effectiveness.

The final aspect of developing the valuing of voice is to build capacity to appreciate and understand diversity of perspectives and beliefs. Not all members of the team will have the same viewpoints and value structures. Leaders do not want teams that have stakeholders that only have one view on an issue. Leaders want a variety of lens so that the discussions on how to meet expectations to achieve the established goals will yield the best possible action plans. If there is a variety of perspectives and a true valuing of diverse voice, then the outcomes of the team will help to create culture that is reflective of the shared mission and vision.

The importance of the climate of voice is how stakeholders work to create mores and norms for sharing and valuing diverse ideas. The climate of voice must be an environment of teammates that are open to different ideas, open to honest discussions and an understanding that not all ideas or perspectives will be turned into action steps. What the stakeholders do need to learn is that the process of sharing did shape group understanding and the development of a shared team lens that is focused on the goals. If the climate of voice is positive and welcoming, then the stakeholders will be agreeable to share and listen to all voices. If the climate of voice is judgmental and accusatory, then stakeholders will become reluctant to share and eventually this will cause the team process to erode and the group will fail.

Building a consensus of voice is the process of gathering diverse stakeholder ideas and perspectives, working to systematically organize these perspectives and create a shared voice related to the action steps and goals. If the stakeholders can work together to create a consensus of voice, it will give each member the knowledge that they contributed to the process of the team and the development of action plans to meet the demands of the goals. Consensus is not yielding collaboration to reduce controversy. Consensus will take some difficult conversations and having the honesty and trust that as the team works it will gather, synthesis and form an agreed-upon belief structure and plan for meeting the goals.

The exchange of ideas, the sharing of experiences and the offering of perspectives is voice in action. It is this dynamic exchange among the stakeholders and the energy that is fostered by these exchanges that will embrace stakeholder lens. It will create a culture valuing voice. The sharing and the trust during these exchanges is voice in action. Leaders want stakeholders to feel that they can share and trust in that the team will honor their voice during the sharing and think processes of the team. Voice in action gives teams a way to process through complexity of thought and idea. It allows the team to embrace the complexity and develop strategies that will meet the requirements of the goals for success. Through these developmental steps stakeholder teams will create an environment of valuing voice with dignity and respect.

To establish an effective voice, the strategy of an organization that is multinational or departmentally diversified will contain a more built-in competitive advantage potential (above and beyond what is achievable through a particular business's own competitive strategy) than any other diversification strategy. There are several competitive advantages to a multinational diversification. First, this strategy allows the company to expand into other markets. The company will be able to become a multinational or global competitor. Second, a company with a multinational diversification strategy is able to improve its strategic fit by expanding into both related and unrelated markets. Finally, a company would be able to better utilize its resources and improve its value chain by increasing its relative market share.

The success of a multinational diversification strategy depends on six advantages. The first advantage is to increase the company's long-term attractiveness into new industries. Operating different strategic business units in different markets will help to increase brand awareness and increase the company's market share in different industries. The combination of successful industries that share the same resources and can enhance the value chain of the umbrella company will provide a stronger return on investment that the company would through its own particular competitive strategy. Companies that diversify into attractive multinational markets will gain an increase in revenue and competitive advantage.

There are several circumstances where an already diversified company might choose to pursue corporate restructuring. The first circumstance is to make sure that the diversified units are meeting their maximum potential.

Whether the company has chosen a related or unrelated diversification strategy, it is important to make sure that the strategy allows the parent company to provide the right amount of assets and finances to help each business unit. In some cases, a company may be operating in multiple markets. While some of the markets may be in the same industry, the products may need to be handled individually and be restructured into a new brand ore business unit. This strategy will help the parent company to strengthen its overall name by improving the individual business units.

The next circumstance that would influence a diversified company to pursue corporate restructuring is to improve the use of technology and other resources. Technology helps diversified companies to further grow and to expand into new markets. The development of new technologies and processes will influence how the company chooses to do business. When the company is diversified into many different markets, it will want to make sure to find the most effective and cost-effective mode of producing goods and services. Technology provides changes to the current business model and also provides new opportunities to the company's value chain.

The third circumstance that would influence a diversified company to pursue corporate restructuring is to transfer its core competencies and assets. The combined use of core competencies and the efficient use of assets will allow the company to improve its synergy among its business units. With diversified companies, the parent company will want to make sure that the different business units work together in order to improve efficiency, lower costs and share leadership and management skills.

Finally, corporate restructuring would help to improve the overall dynamics and performance of a diversified company. Corporate restructuring would improve communication and knowledge of the leaders of the business units and parent company. This strategy would be beneficial to developing an improved management and leadership team. Restructuring the diversified units will create strong leaders in individual markets that will increase the market share and working capital. Corporate restructuring would also lead to the increase of revenue and dividends to shareholders and investors. Restructuring a diversified company will help to unify all aspects of the business increasing its value chain and improve its market share.

There are several merits of strategic alliances and collaborative partnerships for companies racing for global market leadership. The main merit of strategic alliances and collaborative partnerships is to help companies to accelerate the development of new products and technology. The development of new technology and products will help give the collaborative partners a competitive advantage on developing and selling merchandise in a new market giving them a first-mover advantage.

Second, a strategic alliance can help companies to improve their business operations, functions and knowledge. When companies join forces and form an alliance, they both will gain expertise from the other and will be able to improve their supply chain management structure. The companies will be able to lower the level of risk management, increase economies of scale, improve production and increase their marketing resources. A strategic alliance and collaborative partnership can also help companies to sustain tough economic times and to develop a strong competitive advantage in new or existing markets by combining their knowledge and resources.

In order for companies to compete in a global market, it is important for them to develop strong alliances with other countries. This alliance will help to lower operational costs and will also speed up the amount of time needed to enter the new market. In order to enter a new global market, it would be beneficial for a company to form a strategic alliance with another company in that country or market. This strategy would help to lower its costs in the new market and would also help it to form a strong relationship with the government in the new country since it is working to help improve its economy with the strategic alliance.

A strategic alliance would also make sense in a global market when a company wants to lower its operational costs and increase its ability to gain knowledge about the market from an existing competitor. This strategy would allow for the development of new products and services and would help the company to achieve a sustainable competitive advantage and increased market share. A strategic alliance and collaborative partnership would contribute to a competitive advantage in that the amount of operational and financial resources would be increased allowing the company to increase its level of competition. Vertical and horizontal integration would be used to help the company better position itself in the market. This strategy would also allow a company to revolutionize the industry with the development of new products or services. Finally, a strategic alliance in a global economy would allow the company to have more resources to enter untapped markets and to gain a first-mover advantage.

Strategic alliances and collaborative partnerships are also necessary for companies that are racing to seize opportunities in an industry of the future. In order for a company to seize opportunities in the future, it must be able to sustain a competitive advantage in the present. The lower the operational costs, the more revenue and resource the company will have to invest in a future industry. A strategic alliance will allow companies to share their knowledge and to increase its skill base allowing it to strengthen its core competencies.

Strategic alliance and collaborative partnerships make sense when racing to seize opportunities in an industry of the future when trying to lower the level of risk. New and future industries are untapped markets. The industry could prove to be financially profitable or could be a bad business venture. A strategic alliance would help to mitigate the costs and would allow for additional resources to be used in order to ensure its success and to take advantage of the first-mover advantage. The strategic alliance would also help to form a "beachhead" in order to allow the collaborative partnership to limit competition from their competitors ensuring the companies a large market share and return on investment.

Strategic alliances and collaborative partnerships are critical in helping a company to achieve an important objective. First, they help to improve the core competencies making the company stronger and focused on its strategic vision. Second, strategic alliances minimize the threat of outside competition and help to sustain market share. Third, collaborative partnerships will allow companies compete in global or untapped markets that it would not normally have the ability or resources to gain entrance. Fourth, this strategy allows for the development of new technology, products and processes that would revolutionize the industry. Fifth, a collaborative partnership would allow a company to have a proactive approach to competition and become an industry leader instead of being reactive to other companies. Finally, strategic alliances and collaborative partnerships help to increase the opportunities of the company in their market segment by combining all of the resources and capabilities of both companies into one strategic strategy.

There are two strategic management approaches to managing alliances. The first is cost minimization. In cost minimization, a firm must establish contracts with partners and other individuals. The formal contracts are used to monitor and manage the strategic alliance between the firms. This situation is required to eliminate the self-serving interests of both parties involved in the strategic alliance. The second approach to managing alliances is opportunity maximization. Opportunity maximization is used to increase the amount of value-creation in the current business process. Unlike cost minimization, opportunity maximization is a less formal process. There are few constraining requirements for each entity in order to lower costs and increase opportunity. As a result, trust between the businesses is harder to establish. Finally, opportunity maximization is less expensive to implement than cost minimization.

Particularly within small businesses or organizational departments, a "family" atmosphere can develop where coworkers are seen as family or friends. There are special considerations for managing conflict with family and close friends. There are two important dimensions of conflict with any ongoing relationship. In some situations, conflict will rarely arise. When individuals who are family or close friends have a positive relationship, they will be able to understand the needs of each individual. However, when individuals are members of the same family, there is a greater potential for conflict to arise. The individuals involved will have the potential to take advantage of one another based on the predefined relationship.

Second, conflicts between family members and close friends will either be substantive or interpersonal. This type of conflict arises when both parties fail to agree on the tasks or how to resolve a problem. The second form of conflict that can arise between family members and close friends is interpersonal. Interpersonal conflict is when a party interferes with another party's efforts to achieve a specific goal or outcome.

The next special consideration of managing conflict with family and close friends is to develop a level of standards and fairness for each individual. When negotiating with family, the process is more informal as opposed to a formal business contract. The individual might have a better relationship with certain family members than others. This situation can cause the individual to develop different standards for each person under the same contract. As a result, there will be an inconsistent framework and a common ground will not exist between the different parties.

The final consideration of managing conflict with family and close friends is to measure the amount of reciprocity that each member receives. It is important to establishing common norms and behaviors that each member is accountable for following. This strategy will enable the individual to create an equitable level of reciprocity that is based on the results of the outcome instead of the personal relationship with the individual. Implementing an equitable level of reciprocity will enable the individual to create a rewards-based system that will reduce the amount of conflict between family members and close friends within a business or organization.

The team dynamics will impact team and multiparty negotiations. The group dynamics will directly impact the negotiation process. Next, group dynamics are used in team and multiparty negotiations to achieve a unified or shared goal. The behaviors established by the group dynamics will be used to assist in the development of new strategies and processes. As a result, group dynamics will be used to generate new ideas that will lead to alternative dispute resolutions for conflict.

However, group dynamics can also have the potential for dysfunctional team and multiparty negotiations. The first potential for dysfunctional team and multiparty negotiations is simultaneous conversations and over-talking. Individuals within a team or a multiparty can become impatient when they want to have their personal opinion heard by the other members. Instead of listening, an individual may be more focused on what he or she will say. An individual will also begin to talk over the other individuals in order to ensure being heard and understood.

Next, silence and withdrawal can cause a team or multiparty negotiation to become dysfunctional. When there is a large group of people, most individuals will tend to feel insecure about their thoughts and opinions. Instead of expressing their viewpoint, the individual will become shy or withdrawn. The confidence level of the individual will decline causing the individual to not participate in the negotiation process. Finally, an individual will remain silent or withdrawn in a team or multiparty negotiation and defer to the most senior person on the team to make all of the decisions. This situation can cause the senior member of the team to make a decision based on inaccurate or incomplete information since the individual has become silent and has not provided any relevant feedback.

The third potential dysfunctional group dynamic is side conversations. Side conversations occur when individuals on a team or multiparty negotiation will begin whispering or communicating in a private conversation when another member is speaking. This situation can result in information being misunderstood due to a lack of listening or hearing. Next, side conversations can distract the other group members causing the negotiation process to become delayed.

The fourth potential dysfunctional group dynamic is groupthink. Groupthink occurs when an individual may disagree with the decision of the other members but agrees with the majority rule. This situation results from the individual's desire to maintain peace and harmony within the group instead of expressing their true thoughts and opinions. The final potential dysfunctional group dynamic is dominating or blocking. Dominating or blocking occurs in a team or multiparty negotiation when certain individuals will dominate the conversation and prevent others from having the ability to participate. This situation can cause members or the team or party to become frustrated and to withdraw based on the negative persuasion of the dominating member.

There are different strategies and approaches for preventing or managing dysfunctional team dynamics and multiparty negotiations. First, the group dynamics of the team must be established for the team and multiparty negotiations. Second, group dynamics must be used in team and multiparty negotiations to achieve a shared mission or vision in order to keep the group members from getting off track and losing focus of the negotiation. The norms or behaviors established by the group dynamics will be used to assist in the development of new strategies and business processes. As a result, new ideas will be generated by the group members that can lead to alternative solutions for a win-win negotiation.

However, group dynamics must be used as a strategy to prevent any dysfunction in team and multiparty negotiations. The first potential for dysfunctional team and multiparty negotiations is simultaneous conversations and over-talking. Members within a team or multiparty can become impatient when they want to have their personal opinion heard by the other members. Instead of listening, an individual will become focused only on what he or she will choose to voice to the group. An individual will also begin to talk over the other individuals in order to ensure being heard and understood.

Next, silence and withdrawal can cause a team or multiparty negotiation to become dysfunctional and must be avoided. When there is a large group of people, most individuals will tend to feel insecure about their thoughts and opinions. Instead of expressing their viewpoint, the individual will become shy or withdrawn. The confidence level of the individual will decline causing the individual to not participate in the negotiation process.

Finally, an individual will remain silent or withdrawn in a team or multiparty negotiation and defer to the most senior person on the team to make all of the decisions. This situation can cause the senior member of the team to make a decision based on inaccurate or incomplete information since the individual has become silent and has not provided any relevant feedback. In order to correct this source of group dysfunction, the members of the negotiation must create a solid framework for everyone to safely and openly share their opinions in order to contribute to the overall result of the negotiation.

The third potential dysfunctional group dynamic is side conversations. Side conversations occur when individuals on a team or multiparty negotiation will begin whispering or communicating in a private conversation when another member is speaking. This situation can result in information being misunderstood due to a lack of listening or hearing. Next, side conversations can distract the other group members causing the negotiation process to become delayed. A team or multiparty negotiation process must make sure to discourage this sort of behavior in order to maintain a healthy balance between all individuals in the group.

The fourth potential dysfunctional group dynamic is groupthink. Groupthink occurs when an individual may disagree with the decision of the other members but agrees with the majority rule. This situation results from the individual's desire to maintain peace and harmony within the group instead of expressing their true thoughts and opinions. The final potential dysfunctional group dynamic is dominating or blocking. Dominating or blocking occurs in a team or multiparty negotiation when certain individuals will dominate the conversation and prevent others from having the ability to participate. This situation can cause members or team or party to become frustrated and to withdraw based on the negative persuasion of the dominating member. In order to avoid groupthink, the team or multiparty negotiators must promote individual thinking and establish a communication method that allows everyone to share their feelings and thoughts.

To prevent or manage dysfunctional team dynamics in team and multiparty negotiations, there are several processes that can be implemented. The first process is to agree upon an agenda. An agenda is necessary to establish an ordered sequence of items of events that must be completed by the group or team members. In order to establish an effective agenda, it is important that all group members work together to determine the plan for achieving the goals, time and resources that will be required as part of the negotiation.

The second step in the process of preparing for team and multiparty negotiations is to clarify the roles of each member. Specific individuals will need to act as a facilitator, mediator, scribe and timekeeper during the negotiation. The third step is deciding on procedural rules. Procedural rules are important because they will determine how the team or group will initiate and operate the meetings. Finally, the procedural rules that are established will also be used to determine how the conflict experienced during the negotiation will be resolved by all of the team or party members. This situation is important to resolving the issues and keeping a consistent framework.

The fourth step is utilizing public note-taking. Public note-taking is necessary to provide a documented written record of the meeting notes. While individuals will be responsible for keeping their own notes, public notes will be used to express the collective thoughts of the entire team or party members. Failure to keep a log or notes will prevent the group from forming a consensus or having information to reference later in the negotiation process. Fifth, a group or multiparty will want to utilize active listening and also summarize the information on a regular basis. Active listening will help to build trust and establish an open level of communication. Finally, summarizing all of the information will enable the negotiator to clarify the thoughts and opinions of the entire committee for both public and private members.

The sixth process of preparing for team and multiparty negotiations and voiced communication is using a facilitator or mediator. A facilitator or mediator is necessary to help continue to move the negotiation process forward. The facilitator or mediator will also help to resolve any conflict that arises between the team and multiparty members. The seventh process that can be used to prevent dysfunction within a team or multiparty negotiation is to find an early agreement on some issues.

Finding an early agreement on some issues will help create a milestone for the group. This strategy will enable the team members to form a common ground or framework for resolving the more complicated issues that will occur during the negotiation. The eighth process is to use subgroups to secure a tentative agreement. Subgroups will be able to secure a tentative agreement by leaving the main group to focus on a smaller issue. This strategy will also help to save time and resources by conducting different courses of research at the same time. The tentative agreement will then be used as a baseline for the larger group to use in the decision-making process.

The final process of preparing for team and multiparty negotiations is to use caucuses. Caucuses are a form of a "time-out" that enables the group to make adjustments to the decision-making process before continuing with the negotiation process. This strategy is used to help improve the communication between the team and multiparty members. As a result, the team or multiparty negotiations are able to provide a summary or recap of all the work that was done in order to arrive at the final decision for the conflict resolution.

A specific process for developing stakeholder relationships involves six stages. The six stages are assessing the corporate culture, identifying stakeholder groups, identifying stakeholder issues, assessing the organization's commitment to social responsibility, identifying resources and determining urgency, and gaining stakeholder feedback. Assessing the corporate culture is necessary to ensure that the organization has a unified structure and is properly aligned with the strategic mission and vision.

The main purpose of assessing the corporate culture is to consider the impact on social responsibility in relation to the mission and vision of the organization and strategic objectives. The value and norms of a company are very important and should be documented. This situation enables the company to hold every employee accountable for his or her actions. As a result, the company will develop a unified corporate culture focused around the strategic goals and to support the diversified interests of the stakeholders.

The second stage in developing stakeholder relationships is identifying stakeholder groups. Identifying stakeholder groups is important for a company because it enables it to understand the needs of each group of stakeholders. Stakeholder management "is critical to the success of every project in every organization" (Mind Tools, n. d., para. 1). During this stage, the organization will need to identify and distinguish between the primary and secondary stakeholders. The primary stakeholders will need to be considered in the decision-making process and the social responsibility of the company.

The secondary stakeholders are less critical and will not be directly impacted by the initial action of the company. When a company identifies the stakeholder groups, resources can be properly managed. The organization will become more effective and efficient in its business operation. As a result, the company and stakeholders will experience a growth in market share and return on investment.

The third stage in developing stakeholder relationships is identifying stakeholder issues. In order to be successful, an organization must determine the most legitimate and powerful stakeholders. Stakeholders who are viewed as more powerful will be given priority when addressing the needs of the different group of investors. Once needs have been prioritized, the company will need to understand the issues in order to make decisions and implement a business strategy. This situation will enable the company to resolve the issues of the legitimate and powerful stakeholders in order to gain the confidence and support of shareholders while remaining socially responsible.

The fourth stage in developing stakeholder relationships is assessing the organization's commitment to social responsibility. During this stage, the organization is able to develop strategic objectives and goals that match the desired level of social responsibility to the stakeholders and environment. The company will be able to establish tasks, policies and procedures that state the concerns of the primary and secondary stakeholder groups. As a result, the company is able to implement formalized policies and procedures to ensure social responsibility in each step of the company's business process.

The fifth stage in developing stakeholder relationships is identifying resources and determining urgency. Identifying resources and determining urgency is critical to analyzing and determining the allocation of the organization's resources in order to meet the needs of the stakeholders. There are two stages to identifying resources and determining the urgency of the needs of the stakeholders. First, the financial commitment and level of investment during each stage of the business process will need to be understood in order to determine the return on investment. Next, a company will need to realize and prioritize the social responsibilities to ensure that the most urgent and critical issues are given priority to be resolved.

The final stage in developing stakeholder relationships is gaining stakeholder feedback within the "clear" lens of the organization. Stakeholder feedback is important to the evaluation of the satisfaction of the stakeholder's needs. When stakeholders provide positive feedback, the company has been successful at meeting the critical needs. However, negative feedback from stakeholders will cause the company to change its business strategy in order to improve performance and satisfaction. Stakeholder feedback from stakeholders can be collected through a variety of different ways. First, feedback can be collected through the results of surveys. The information the stakeholders provide through surveys will help the company to make improvements to meeting the various needs.

Second, a company can gain feedback through different media and online resources that include websites, blogs, articles and newsletters. Third, the company can provide focus groups for its stakeholders. This situation will enable the company to understand the needs of the individual stakeholder groups better and to develop a more effective business strategy to meet their needs. The main goal of the process of developing stakeholder relationships is to establish a high level of communication and trust between the top management and various stakeholder groups of the company. When there is a high level of communication and trust, the company will become more socially responsible and able to meet the needs of the different investors and stakeholders.

The fourth stage is the most important part of the process of developing stakeholder relationships. Assessing the organization's commitment to social responsibility is the most important stage in this process because it determines the success of the company's ability to coordinate the corporate culture with the identified stakeholder groups and issues. Before a company invests raw materials and financial resources into a business strategy, it will need to make sure that it has made the right commitment to become socially responsible based on the needs of the stakeholders and economy. However, stakeholder feedback is also an important step in the process of developing relationships. Since every action of a company is to be socially responsible and to maximize the profit of its shareholders, the level of satisfaction provided from the stakeholders will be crucial in determining the appropriate business strategy. This situation will help to provide open communication and trust between the top management and stakeholders within the company.

As a result, the company will experience a high level of loyalty and improved reputation in the market. The company will be able to meet the needs of the stakeholder and implement the necessary measure to the business process to remain socially responsible. The part of the process of developing stakeholder relationships that seems most difficult is identifying the stakeholder groups. Within a company, each group of stakeholder believes that their needs are the most important. The company must logically determine the importance and organizational impact of the needs of the stakeholders before implementing a business strategy. This situation will be most difficult for the company based on the different and unique needs, wants and desires of each stakeholder.

The importance of voice is a belief in diversity of perceptions and an open culture that embraces all the different viewpoints offered by the stakeholders. It is because of the diversity of viewpoints and how the leaders structure a system that welcomes diverse perspectives that will ensure that the best possible outcomes are derived from the work of the stakeholders. This belief in diversity of lens and voice becomes the foundation of interactions among stakeholders. The leader is the measure of how this is being implemented in the schools. The leader must first learn to honor and value their own voice.

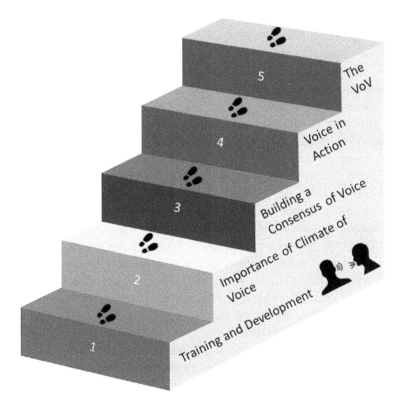

**Figure 4** Stepping up to voice.

Have faith in their lens and beliefs. It is through this understanding of self that a leader can then begin to model and demonstrate the valuing of diversity among stakeholder's lens and voice. The leader must be confident in their ability to lead and to engage. They also must be comfortable not leading. That for true shared leadership to be part of the operating system of the school, leaders need to yield leadership to other stakeholders. They should be confident enough in their skills as leaders and comfortable in their position as leaders to give up control and allow others to lead.

In valuing the importance of voice, this is an important concept that must be internalized by leaders. The most powerful leaders are those that can give up part of the operational leadership and truly give importance to voice. Giving space for stakeholder voice to be a driving force is necessary to help move the team forward. This is difficult for many leaders. Giving up control can be scary. Will the other members of the team keep the group focused and moving forward or will the dynamic falter and fragment the team? Will conflict among stakeholders cause the team to fail and not meet its goals? These are real concerns for leaders. What the leader chooses to do will reveal if they believe in the importance of voice. The development of professional learning that will allow stakeholders to hone their skills in shared leadership and in valuing the importance of voice will be an important step for the team dynamic. It is this collective understanding and belief that divergent voice is important and can be a benefit to the overall success of the team and school.

Connecting stakeholder experience and the mission and vision of the organization will allow members to access their developed skills and further enhance the dynamic of the team. The collective wisdom of the members is far greater than the singular wisdom of the leader. There is vastly more experience and significant depth of understanding that has been developed through time and trial. To not access this expertise would limit the scope of understanding of the issues for the leader and the team. By accessing these experiences, the leader can relinquish leadership to the other members of the team, allow those with expertise and experience to drive direction toward meeting the established goals. By accessing the collective wisdom and garnering a shared understanding of experiences, the decision-making process will have greater success because of the depth and breadth of information that was used in making a final choice.

By accessing collective experience and wisdom, the team can commit to each other. Each stakeholder has a responsibility to commit to the team norms and to demonstrate trust and respect of each member. How the team coordinates their work and how the stakeholders embrace their role is part of the process of committing to the work of the team. The social interactions and the dynamic of the exchanges are part of the shared leadership and valuing of voice process. Stakeholders have a social responsibility to act in the best interests of the team, not in their own best interests that could be detrimental to the success of the group.

When addressing the importance of voice, it is important to help develop skills in how to listen to divergent viewpoints of stakeholders. Too often, members of a team hear the members of the group but did not reflect or engage with what was said. The stakeholder hears what their team member said, but they did not really listen. The leader must also be mindful that they stay in a place of listening to the stakeholders and not to fall into a default of hearing. How to ensure that stakeholders are listening is to institute a practice of paraphrasing and repeating what a stakeholder just shared. Additionally, it is a good strategy to share how the perspective that was offered is valued and is important to the overall development process of the team.

The leader can establish, with collaboration with the stakeholders on the team, a set of listening expectations. How the team will actively listen to each member who took the risk to share. If the team is to value the importance of voice, then all voices are valuable. One expectation that must be done with clarity is that not all shared perspectives may end up in the final action plan developed by the team to address the goals. It is important for stakeholders to share and have trust in the process. The leader must ensure not only that each stakeholder's voice is valued but also that there will be a refinement process that may combine and cull shared information together to develop one synthesized action plan.

As the stakeholders develop their skills at listening, they also must embrace the fact that there will be a diversity of perspectives. Stakeholders due to their past experiences and lens have a diverse collection of backgrounds that can have a positive impact on the work of the team. The notion of diversity must be viewed as a strength of the team, and the sharing of a vast array of different ideas and viewpoints is how the best solutions will be developed. The demographics of each stakeholder will also create diversity of perspectives. How each stakeholder views the interactions of the team and how they embrace these different viewpoints will be a critical aspect of how successful the team will be in reaching its goals. The leader with the stakeholders will need to develop a working plan on how to celebrate diversity and use these diverse perspectives to strengthen outcomes and action plans.

In this process of celebrating diversity and embracing a wide range of perspectives, the leader and the stakeholders must reduce conflict and the "noise" that will cloud the focus of the work of the team. It is important to celebrate diverse perspectives, but it is also important to keep the team focused on the goals and meeting the expectations of these goals. The distractions that the noise can cause could derail the team and cause the team to become caught into fixes that fail. The team must remain moving forward to accomplish their goals. Noise becomes a distraction that will cause the team to lose momentum, and if they fall into fixes that fail, the outcomes the team develops will not address the needs of the organization. In this process, teachers experience noise; they are bombarded by a variety of agendas that are not in the best interest of the team or the organization. If the team can remain focused and use diverse perspectives to think through every option, then the distracting noise will not negatively impact the work of the team.

# Chapter 4

# LEADERS LENDING VOICE

Several significant studies have demonstrated that leaders of behavioral organizations use a variety of strategies to shape and move decision-making. Many of the leadership methodologies focus on the skillfulness of the leader and how the actions of the leader will shape direction of the organization or the school. How influential and powerful leaders can impact change is due to their influence. These studies also outlined key tenets that leaders should follow to maximize their effectiveness. Machiavelli shared that it is better for leaders to be feared than to be loved. The idea was a separation between those that lead and those that follow. That is if a leader is not loved, there will be an erosion of the respect and those that are to follow will begin to question the authority of the leader.

More current leadership theories expanded on the skills that leaders need to possess to be effective. Leaders need to have operational expertise of the organization or school. They need to understand the variety of departments within the organization as well as be charismatic and personable. These theories focused on the leader and their ability to lead, not truly how to engage others into leadership roles. The foundation of leadership authority is not in the ability to control all variables, but to use the stakeholders within and around the organization to help facilitate a network of support to help address the multiple variables that are significant in any decision that will drive change. Leaders need to foster stakeholder voice and embrace the release of task-specific leadership to members of the team to ensure that the goals of the organization are addressed.

Yukl (2010) states that there are three main types of leadership behavioral methodologies: task-oriented, relations-oriented and change-oriented. These three broad leadership behaviors address the skills and talents of the leader as the driving force for organization growth and improvement. Task-oriented leadership focuses on the processes needed to ensure that all members of the team are focused on the goals and associated responsibilities. There is a need to bring order and structure to the actions of the team to improve efficiency and effectiveness (Yukl, 2010). The challenge with this type of leadership is that in the drive to be effective and efficient there is a loss of voice among the stakeholders. There is a limiting of exchanges and time that stifles the variety of voice and the discussion of varying perspectives that comes from using the collective wisdom of the stakeholders.

The counter to this is that leaders need to embrace the fact that the process of working toward goal-oriented solutions may become "messy" or convoluted and that the discussions among the stakeholders and the valuing of voice may take time. This addition of time may reduce efficiency and may reduce focus on specific tasks. The positive aspects of the leader lending voice to the stakeholders is that through these discussions, better resolutions and solutions are discovered that will better address reaching the established goals. By reducing the rigor of task-oriented leadership, the leader will be open to a focus on outcomes and long-term systems and then the task steps that will create quick fixes that fail. A focus on task and not outcomes, a practice of task efficiency and not growth discussions, reduces the influence of voice and reduces the engagement and ownership of the decision-making for all stakeholders.

Relation-oriented leadership is focused on developing the social and psychological aspects of the teams (Bergman et al., 2012). The development of the connective threads that intertwine the stakeholders to the process and the completion of the goals is the important aspect of relation-oriented leadership. The leader's behaviors will move this type of leadership forward. Leaders will appear to be friendly, supportive, respectful and concerned for the well-being of the stakeholders involved in the shared leadership (Bergman et al., 2012). Relation-oriented leadership behaviors also include resolving conflicts, providing encouragement and ensuring that all members' opinions are heard (Bergman et al., 2012).

The challenge with simply focusing on relations-oriented leadership is that the leader, not the team, address conflicts or disagreements among the stakeholders. In any team dynamic, there will be conflict and disagreement; how the team develops these processes to address these conditions is important to eventually create meaningful collaborative decisions that are focused on the established goals. Developing relationships is important, creating the common threads that connect stakeholders to each other and their work is a powerful tool to help foster a dynamic team environment; however, it cannot be the sole process of connecting the stakeholders to the process or the goals.

Change-oriented leadership behaviors are oriented toward change, improving strategic decisions, adapting to change, increasing innovation and fostering commitment to visions and goals (Yukl, 2010). Envisioning leaders create new and compelling visions that help to facilitate idea generation, define overall goals and encourage others to view issues in a different way

(Bergman et al., 2012). They draw others into the envisioning process and foster group ownership of central ideas (Bergman et al., 2012).

For many, change is an uncomfortable process. They do not like change, nor do they want to be part of a process that brings change. Most people would be willing to remain in their current systems even though they know that the current system is not the most optimal for their work. It is because of comfort. To drive change is always a balancing act of those who embrace change and those who resist change. Being a change-oriented leader, creating a new mission and vision that will allow for new ideas and new systems can be a powerful tool in leadership. It sets the stage for the behavioral organization operating environment that seeks new ideas and new thinking. In the process this style of leadership can alienate stakeholders and make them feel that their opinions and perceptions are not important.

In today's complex environment of shifting demands and requirements of behavioral organizations and school, the need for leadership to create an environment where stakeholders are valued and the expertise they possess is viewed as highly desirable to help further develop the organization or the school. Developing a leadership model that connects these three types of leadership allows the stakeholders to see that their voice is valued and that the leaders of the organization are lending voice to all stakeholders. In today's organizations, where success depends on effectively integrating the knowledge of skilled professionals in complex and ambiguous environments, it is becoming increasingly unlikely that a single, vertical leader will possess all of the knowledge, abilities and skills required to fulfill all of the necessary leadership roles (Bergman et al., 2012). Leadership responsibilities should shift according to which member's expertise is most relevant to the task at hand (Friedrich et al., 2009). Stakeholders as well as leaders may have a preference for one style of leadership over the others, but to create real ownership and value of voice, leaders need to embrace all three types of leadership. Previous research has supported the notion that different leader behaviors are independent (Yukl, 2010), suggesting that performing one type of leader behavior does not guarantee being inclined to perform any other type. Thus, a single individual may be unwilling and/or unable to fulfill all of the necessary leadership tasks of the team (Bergman et al., 2012).

Creating a leadership model that will embrace shared leadership responsibilities and foster an environment where all voice is valued and important should be the task of all stakeholders on the team. Stakeholders, once they agree on the norms and structure of the team dynamic, hold each other accountable for how each member operates within the team. How each stakeholder's voice is valued and incorporated into the discussion of how to meet the expectations of the goal. Shared leadership enables stakeholders to act on their skills and strengths to help better serve the team. They assume situational leadership based on where they feel that they can offer the most support to meet the expectations of the goals. The leader must lend support to all stakeholders' voice to ensure that through open exchanges of ideas the team can consider all information and perspectives to help move the team forward toward insightful decision-making and successfully reaching the expectations and goals that were developed at the on-set of the shared leadership process.

How leaders can move to a shared leadership process requires a clear plan of engagement and activation of all stakeholders. The leader has to create an environment where all stakeholders can help in the development of shared vision. During this process, the leader must lend value to stakeholder voice as well as establish value in their voice. What the leader says and how they say it will shape interactions and exchanges among all stakeholders. If the leader builds a system where stakeholders have concept freedom and have support and guidance from the leader, then what is developed will truly be shared vision.

Once the stakeholders and the leader have created a shared vision, they can begin the work of thinking about what and how to solve the identified issues and meet the expectations of the goals. The process of thinking is to open the discussion to the varied voices that each stakeholder brings to the team. Empowering discussion and use of a critical lens to assess the significance of the perceptions and perspectives that will shape outcomes. The thinking process is an important time for leaders to lend voice to the stakeholders of the team. During this process of thinking, the stakeholders are developing an operating culture. A culture that allows for shared leadership and the valuing of voice for each stakeholder.

Culture is a complex process for leaders to support the team stakeholders through as part of the team dynamic. Team culture and organizational culture might have some different aspects based on the interactions of the stakeholders. Organizational culture has historical foundations based on prior experiences of the organization and the stakeholders. As the organization transforms, the prior culture becomes ineffective, and the void has to be filled with a new culture. The work of the team and the interactions of the stakeholders allows for the development of a new team culture. The valuing of voice of each stakeholder and the shared leadership employed by the team creates a culture of shared respect and understanding. The further the team works toward the established goals, the more refined the culture becomes and is reflective of the shared values of the stakeholders. The team culture can impact the organization culture. The more success the team has on supporting each stakeholder and successfully working toward the established goals, the rest of the organization will begin to assume some of the team culture.

Organizational culture gives structure to the process of how the stakeholders develop their shared mission. The mission of the organization allows stakeholders to create and work toward the goals that the team has identified as being a priority. The mission of the organization helps to set direction, the leader must offer a means for stakeholders to embrace the mission and use it to help focus their work toward meeting the expectations of the goals. Mission is a unifying message and a set of beliefs that bind the stakeholders to a common value system. Leaders have to ensure that each stakeholder has voice in the process of developing the mission as well as understanding how the mission impacts the varied systems that operate within the organization.

A well-defined and transparent mission that is embedded in the culture of a behavioral organization supports the collective actions outlined by the shared leadership team. The mission and culture create an environment that values voice and give importance to the many different perceptions each stakeholder brings to their work. From this, organizations and schools create action plans that address the process of growth toward their goals. As leaders support the development of these action plans, it is important for the organization and the stakeholders to become reflective leaders and assess results. Did the plan developed by the stakeholders and the leader address the issues and the goals established at the beginning of their work? The examination of results is important. Outcomes drive improvement and growth. The leader has to have a system that allows stakeholders to be able to put a critical lens to what they have done. How their actions have impacted success toward their goals, how has their plans improved the organization or school helps in the examining results is the process of being reflective. Rooting next steps in the study of results ensures that the stakeholders do not get caught in a loop of fixes that fail. The leader and the stakeholders can assess and keep what worked while moving to change what did not work. It is by assessing results and examining if the outcomes match the expected goals of the team. From this examination, the stakeholders can then embark on a new vision process and start the shared leadership team process again to continue the improvement of the organization.

There are several different things company executives need to do to lead the strategy-execution process. First, company executives need to develop and implement a strategy that is action-oriented and is driven by business operations. The executives will need to make sure that the strategy-execution process is implemented by the managers so they can determine what the company must do differently in order to improve the overall quality of production. Once the problems within the organization are identified, the company executives will need to set up new internal policies and regulations in order to address the issues within the corporation.

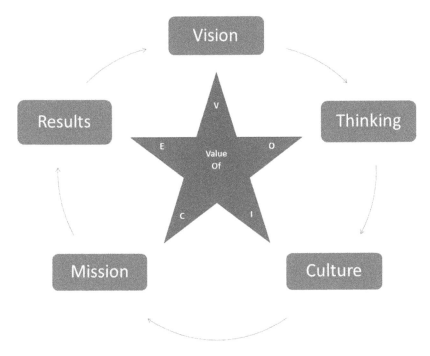

**Figure 5** The five points of voice.

Next, company executives would need to develop a team effort among the employees. It is critical that every employee becomes an active participant in the strategy-execution process. Employees must be able to visualize the strategy in order to become part of the organization's team. When the employee has a "what's in it for me" mentality, they are more willing to becoming involved in the team effort. As a result, the strategy-execution process will be implemented and carried out to completion.

Company executives will need to make sure that the company has staffed the organization with the right people. People are a company's most important asset and are important for executing strategy. Next, the core capabilities would need to be determined. Company executives would need to make sure to include any additional capabilities in the strategy execution. Third, the executives would need to create a supportive organizational structure. The structure of the organization is a critical component to executing strategy. Placing employees in the right positions and "right sizing" the organization will help to better execute the overall strategy.

Fourth, resources will need to be properly allocated. Company executives will want to make sure that managers and every department has an accurate budget in order to execute the strategy. Fifth, supportive policies and procedures would need to be established. Employees are resistant to change. Executives will want to remove any obstacles of resistance to change in order to proceed with the execution of strategy. Failure to eliminate this obstacle will cause the strategy to not be implemented. Next, new policies and procedures that support the strategy-execution process will be crucial in making the strategy work.

Sixth, executives will need to ensure that the company adopts processes for continuous improvement. Six Sigma and establishing a high benchmark for quality control will ensure the success of strategy implementation. Seventh, new systems will need to be integrated in order to increase the efficiency of the company's core competencies and business model. Eight, company executives will need to develop a reward program that motivates the employees. Intrinsic and extrinsic incentives should be established to reward employees for only the right behavior in order to comply with the company's code of conduct.

Ninth, the right corporate culture would need to be determined. Culture is important in becoming an ally to the execution of the company's strategy. Corporate culture helps to bring every employee together as a cohesive unit. Finally, internal leadership will be needed by the executives in order to move the strategy forward. A strong leadership and management team is critical in setting the example and motivating the employees to execute the company's strategic process and vision.

In order for executives to lead the strategy-execution process, it is important to utilize and build upon the core capabilities of the company. The development of a strong internal value chain will help the executives to execute the desired strategy. Company executives will also need to recognize that employees are the main resource for the company and should use them to help with new innovation and business processes. Executives will also need to structure the organization based on the needs of the new strategy. Finally, executives will need to implement a strong reward system in order to motivate their employees to support the implementation and execution of the company's strategy.

There are primary aspects of the strategic management process. The strategic management process also enables a firm to increase its profit and earn above-average returns for its shareholders. Before a firm can gain a competitive advantage in the market, the senior management team must develop a business plan. Next, the company must implement the new strategy and to gain the support of the various groups of investors. Finally, the strategic management process has five different stages that include goal setting, analysis, strategy formation, strategy implementation and strategy monitoring.

The first stage of the strategic management process is goal setting. During the goal-setting phase, the organization must first state the short-term and long-term goals and objectives that must be achieved. Next, goal setting requires that the organization establishes a business process in order to succeed in completing stated goals and objectives. Finally, goal setting will state the mission and strategic vision of the company.

The second stage of the strategic management process is analysis. Analysis is an important part of the strategic management process because it allows the organization to gather and review all of the relevant information required to make a strategic decision. This situation enables the senior managers to understand the current and future needs of the organization. As a result of the analysis, the company will be able to develop a customized strategy that will support its overall mission and vision. The third stage is strategy formulation. Strategy formulation is used to analyze and determine what resources and assets will be required to achieve the strategic vision.

The fourth stage is strategy implementation. Strategy implementation is used to analyze the success of the current structure and business operation. If the current structure is insufficient in sustaining long-term stability, changes and alternative courses of action will be required to improve the strategic plan. The final stage of the strategic management process is evaluation and control. Evaluation and control are required to review the results of the strategy. Parameters and performance measures are implemented to measure the project expectations with the actual results of the strategic plan.

There is a direct relationship between the strategic management process and organizational ethics. The strategic management process utilizes ethics to satisfy and meet the needs of the various stakeholder groups. Ethics will be used to determine how a company will operate and compete against its competitors. A company can be determined to have an ethical strategy in several different ways. First, the company's strategy must be legal. If the actions of the company are not abiding by the laws of the government, then the strategy cannot be ethical.

Second, a company's strategy is ethical if it holds to the core values of its founder or CEO. All actions of an organization must be for the good of the entire company. Ethics are created in a top-down approach within an organization. If the actions of the CEO and top managers are unethical or unmoral, the result will be that the entire company will become unethical. Actions cannot be self-serving for a single department, manager or employee. Every action must be for the success and benefit of the entire company. Ethical leaders are important for a company when establishing its long-term strategic management process.

There are certain actions leaders must do to develop and sustain an effective organizational culture. The culture of an organization creates a social norm for the employees and allows consumers to know what they can expect from the company. The behavior of an organization determines how it will respond to the needs of the consumers and the surrounding business environment. The structure and culture of the organization are how it is able to achieve its goals.

Organizational theory, organizational design and change and organizational structure and interrelated to each other. Together, each area works together to help form a cohesive business structure and strategic plan. Organizational theory and design create the social norm for a formal and informal organization. The business processes and use of resources can be properly managed. The organization's human resources and level of communication at every level are also improved with a strong structure, design and theory. Finally, business functions, organizational and consumer behavior, products and services and business markets can be managed to meet the changing needs of the consumer with organizational theory, organizational design and change and organizational structure.

Next, organizational culture is defined by a combination of ideologies, symbols and core values that provide the framework for the company. The core values are shared by each employee and member of the top management team. Next, organizational framework will determine how the company conducts its business operations. This situation will enable a company to use its organizational structure to add value to its value chain to and to create a competitive advantage within the product market.

However, it is difficult to change the core values and culture of an organization. As a result, most organizations will sustain the original culture established by the top management team. In order to implement effective leadership, the firm must be able to recognize the need for organizational change. Organizational change is the method an organization uses to transfer from its current state of business operation to its desired level. Organizational change helps to increase the efficiency and effectiveness of the organization.

Organizational change and design is important at all levels within the organization. The management of organizational and design allows management to control all activities and functions of the business process. Next, organizational change and design balance the needs of the organization. Within every organization, it is important to understand the internal and external needs. Organizations that are able to control internal and external needs are able to increase their revenue, increase return on investment and continue to compete in the future.

Next, organizational change can be established through incremental changes when implementing a new strategy. However, drastic changes to the organizational culture can occur in order to break away from the original strategy that provided a historical framework for the company. In order to gain support of the change within the organization, the firm will need to communicate the new values of the firm to recruit individuals who have the right values and are able to provide innovative solutions to existing problems. Finally, organizations will need to select new individuals who are able to share the same culture and values in order to support the strategic vision and mission of the top management team and board of directors.

The reputation of an organization takes a long time to create and develop. An organization's reputation is determined by its success to satisfy the needs of the consumer market and the stakeholders. Every action and decision made by the company should be done to create a positive image and increase the loyalty and support of the stakeholders. In today's global economy, reputation management is very important to the success of a company. When a company has a positive image or reputation, its goods and services become more accepted and desired within the market. However, a negative corporate image will cause a company to experience a loss in sales, investments by stakeholders and an increased amount of risk in the industry or market segment.

Reputation management is affected by different and changing trends in the economic environment. A company must change the way it manages its reputation based on the current needs of the market. There are various market variables a company must consider when managing its reputation. The first variable is the increased knowledge of consumers based on technology and improved accessibility to product information. Second, the factors of the workplace such as rewards, safety and culture will need to be considered. Third, the company's link between the distributors, vendors and suppliers will need to be monitored in order to maintain long-term relationship.

Finally, the reputation management of an organization will be determined by the employees. When the employees are valued and fully integrated into the company, productivity and quality will increase. This situation will create a positive long-term reputation for the company. However, failure to gain the support of employees will lead to an immediate short-term decline in the company's reputation. As a result, the company will experience an immediate need for change in order to make improvements to the business process and to maximize the profits of stakeholders.

As a result, the organizational reputation will be formed based on the perception of the stakeholders and will determine in type of ethical action and social responsibility it has within the environment. It is important to manage these elements in order to ensure that the company properly manages its reputation. Failure to maintain a good reputation will result in the need for crisis management. This situation will deplete the resources and finances of the company causing a decrease in shareholder profit and market share.

The notion that leadership is a process is based on the belief that the right leaders will emerge based on certain factors that are defined by a given situation. The leader, follower and context of the situation will vary from each situation. Since every situation is different, there will always be a different outcome based on the events. The leadership process is bounded by a framework of different interlocking factors that include a leader, follower and context. Within the leadership process, the people and situation will undergo dynamic and complex changes in events.

There are five dynamic variables within the leadership process. The first variable in the leadership process is the leader. The leader is defined as the person who oversees and takes charge of the specific action in the environment. The second variable is the followers. Followers are the individuals who follow the direction set forth by the leader. The third variable is the context. The context is the situation that surrounds the leaders. The level of complexity and formal structure will depend on the complexity of the environment. The fourth variable is the process. The process involves the leading and following of individuals within the act of leadership. The process is critical to determining the guidance and developing the relationships to obtain the stated goal or objective. The final variable is the outcome. An outcome is the end result that occurs from the linked interactions of variables during the leadership process. The outcome is the level of success of relationship between the individuals or groups of people involved in the activity.

The leadership process has four different stages. During the first stage, the group within the given environment has an emotional or practical need that is essential to address. The first stage of the leadership process will help to determine exactly what the problem or opportunity is so the appropriate action can be determined. During the second stage of the leadership process, the leader must respond to the event or activity. The action of the leader must represent the entire population involved in the activity.

The third stage of the leadership process focuses on the results of the behavior. The responses provided by the leader and their leadership are analyzed and classified into categories. This strategy allows the implementation of the knowledge, skill and style of the leader to be compared to the needs of the given situation. The final stage of leadership is to assign a name or label to each trait or response of the leader. As a result, the leader is assigned a psychological profile in order to define the individual as a leader in the given context. The leadership process will determine the leadership style of a person in a certain situation and to better understand the conceptualization and emerging roles that are required for the success of the situation.

Charismatic leadership emerges through the LMX process when the variables of a situation cause an individual to come forth and influence the other group members. When an organization is operating in an environment with a complex situation, a leader with necessary skills, abilities and charisma will be determined to guide the group of followers. However, the actions of the followers are based on the extraordinary abilities and gifts of the leader instead of their own thoughts on the mission.

The charisma of a leader is a "gift" and natural ability of an individual to influence, guide and lead other followers. Charismatic leaders are innovative and have a unique way of inspiring other individuals to successfully complete the objective or goal. This situation causes the leader to become innovative and creative instead of only maintaining the status of the situation in the environment. A charismatic leader is able to use their charisma or charm in support and relationship to the mission or strategic vision. Next, a charismatic leader will emerge based on the individual's ability to effectively communicate their vision and beliefs. The success of a charismatic leader depends on role modeling, image building, goal definition, exhibiting confidence and motivating followers in the social environment of an organization.

Charisma and charismatic leadership are also relational in nature. Leadership cannot exist without a leader and a follower. In order for a leader to become charismatic, the individual must develop characteristics, traits and behaviors based on the needs of the current situation. This strategy will enable the leader to influence the followers and to gain their emotional support in order to achieve the strategic vision and goal achievement. Next, a leader can only be charismatic when he or she possesses a high level of self-confidence, influence, dominance and moral righteousness in their actions. Depending on the situation, the unique traits, characteristics, knowledge and past performance will be used to determine the leader.

Charisma is relational in nature through the transformational leadership process. With the transformational leadership process, a leader is able to use his or her charisma in order to model or mold the behavior traits of the group of followers. This situation will cause the followers to share the same feelings and beliefs as the leader in order to obtain the stated goal or objective. Only when the leader has the support and belief from the followers can charismatic leadership exist. Finally, charisma is relational in nature because, based on the traits of the leaders, not all followers will be influenced by the leader's actions. As a result, the observations and perceptions of the followers will determine the success of a leader and his or her ability to use charisma as part of the leadership process.

Knowledge management can promote organizational learning. A knowledge management can provide an effective way of communicating and providing information. As the ability of knowledge to be communicated increases, the quality of information will also improve. Standard Operating

Procedures (SOPs) will be established, allowing real-time information and data to be communicated throughout the organizational hierarchy.

Next, knowledge management will promote organizational learning by providing a cognitive structure. A cognitive structure is a system of shared interrelated values and expectations between the organization and employees in order to efficiently and effectively define an event or a problem within the environment. However, the type of knowledge system will need to be determined based on the individual needs of the organization and the complexity of the environment.

With a tall or mechanistic organization, there is a great deal of structure and standardization. Organizational knowledge is gathered, analyzed and stored into a database retrieval system. The organization is able to use a codification approach when the different functions and divisions are able to provide related and standard information about consumers and products. With a flat and organic organization, the structure of the organization is unstructured. The culture promotes change and innovation to problems. Organic organizations will need to use the personalization approach to knowledge management. Employees in organic organizations must rely heavily on personal insight and use their judgment to make quick business decisions.

With the use of codification or personalization approach, organizations will be able to become specialized in its business environment. With knowledge management and organizational learning, top management will be able to focus on specific products and services in order to increase its value chain and gain market share within the environment. Organizations will need to adopt a knowledge management system based on the knowledge of its employees. Top management must also determine the amount of standardization or innovation that is required to implement the right knowledge management system to incorporate into its culture and structure.

School leaders must develop strategies to enact shared leadership within the organization and engage stakeholders in the decision-making process. School leaders need to identify the strengths among the stakeholders and capitalize on their abilities to be impact members of the team. How the school leader identifies the talents and strengths of the stakeholders and shares with the members of the team where each member has specific skills that will help the progress of the team is an important leadership skill that must be used to benefit the organization. The strategies that engage stakeholders also must protect these same stakeholders when they assume a leadership role. In normal circumstances, stakeholders are viewed as peers and colleagues. There is protection and security when members of the team share the same role and level of responsibilities. As members of the team assume leadership responsibilities, how the team views them will change. It is the leader who must reassure the stakeholder taking the leadership risk as well as the other team members.

Another strategy that leaders need to develop is how to create a true team dynamic. The structure and operational tasks that allow a team to work effectively is critical for their success. How the leader goes about sharing the vision of the team, the associated roles and the collective outcomes that must be achieved by the team. The team atmosphere and the ability of each member to operate within the structures of the team is an important responsibility of the leader. Shared leadership works best in a system where members feel comfortable taking risks. The members must believe that when they take a risk to lead or share perspective, they will be respected and protected. The leader must be the one who sets these expectations and shares these same expectations with the members of the team. The leader is also the person responsible to ensure that the team members follow the agreed-upon rules and structures that will make the team successful.

School leaders must gather organizational information to help set direction and ensure that the mission and vision of the school are in line with the agreed-upon goals. The school leader will need to engage groups of stakeholders to ask probing questions and gather their feedback. The school leader models the valuing of voice and honors the individual lens of each stakeholder as part of the information gathering process. The leader must also protect the stakeholders who took the risk to share their perspectives and understandings of how the school environment operates. It is this skill of keeping confidence and openly asking questions and gathering response data that will help to shape future decisions.

School leaders also must set the conditions that allow the organization's stakeholders to help in setting direction. The lens of each stakeholder and their interactions within the organization are unique to each member. It is the collection of these unique perspectives and organizing the findings from the inquiry process, the leader can begin to set direction. There must be transparency in how the leader came to set the organizational priorities and directions as the members work to meet their goals. Organizational direction and goals will allow stakeholders to work on continuous improvement of the school. The opportunity to risk in an environment that protects the members and celebrates diversity of voice is an essential responsibility of an effective leader.

The style that a leader engages in to gather stakeholders and glean information critical to the continued success of the school is personal to each person. However, charisma is essential for leaders to be able to connect with stakeholders. Within the conditions of shared leadership, the leader must make meaningful connections with the stakeholders. It is through these connections that the leader can build trust and an environment that celebrates risk. The interpersonal skills that engage members in conversations and displays a genuine interest in the stakeholders allows the leader to build bonds that will help to connect people with tasks. It is through these connections that a leader can determine which stakeholders should undertake tasks and focus on specific goals.

Knowledge and understanding of the school environment, the complex dynamics that are part of the operational systems and the beliefs that each stakeholder are some of the most complex leadership skills that a leader must master. Schools are complex systems where multiple stakeholders at multiple levels are operating in concentric spheres that allow the school to support the needs of its most important stakeholders, the students. Leaders must build capacity within themselves to be active learners and engaged listeners to maximize their understanding of the school organization. From this process of shared voice, where each stakeholder has been valued and respected, there will yield a more honest depiction of the strengths and weaknesses of the school and the areas that must be addressed to better serve the students and honor the efforts and work of the teachers. Leaders are obligated to put forth the time and effort to make sure that the understanding they developed of the school environment and culture is based on accurate and varied perspectives from a multitude of stakeholders. It is this reflective behaviors and supportive leadership that will allow all stakeholders to flourish during the continued improvement and the reaching of the shared goals.

As leaders validate voice and embrace the shared leadership process, they need to be clear on how they are releasing leadership to their stakeholders. How will leaders release leadership to teachers, staff, community and students? How do these stakeholders access leadership, and is the leader comfortable in the releasing process? Leaders need to realize that by releasing leadership to stakeholders and empowering them to lead, they solidify their leadership and create a dynamic that strengthens their position within the organization. By creating a more diverse interaction of leading, the team, organization and/ or school will benefit from accessing the abilities and strengths of each stakeholder in the process of continuous improvement.

## References

Bergman, J., Bergman, S., Davenport, S., & Small, E. (2012). The shared leadership process in decision-making teams. *The Journal of Social Psychology, 152*(1), 17–42. http://doi.org/10.1080/00224545.2010.538763

Friedrich, T. L., Vessey, W. B., Schuelke, M. J., Ruark, G. A., & Mumford, M. D. (2009). A framework for understanding collective leadership: The selective utilization of leader and team expertise within networks. *The Leadership Quarterly, 20*, 933–958.

Yukl, G. (2010). *Leadership in organizations* (7th ed.). Prentice Hall.

# Chapter 5

# EMPOWERING EMPLOYEES IN VOICE

This chapter analyzes how shared leadership influences team function and the valuing of employee voice. In organizations and schools, it is common for an employee to feel that they are not heard and that the issues that impact their ability to complete their work are not being addressed and, in many cases, being ignored. It also examines how leaders build systems to be those that value the voice of all stakeholders and specifically employees. Employees have a unique perspective on the operation of an organization or a school. They are the ones doing the work. They can see if systems are not optimal, or policies restrict their ability to efficiently complete their assigned tasks. Therefore, there are real needs within organizations to create an environment that empowers employee voice.

Leaders who use direct decision-making to recommend changes within an organization limit the range and scope of influence that can help with developing outcomes. Direct decision-making removes the ability of stakeholders and most importantly employee from offering feedback and insight into how choices can be made to better the organization. Employees have a unique insight into the operations of an organization or a school. They see practices in place from a different lens than the leader. Their ability to assess operations from the lens of doing the work gives leaders valuable experiential background that can help them to make better decisions. It is the leader's responsibility to foster and value the voice of the employees.

However, if the leaders shift the ability for direct decision-making to the stakeholders, giving specifically employees voice in the process, the decision-making process can be more effective in addressing the goals of the organization. If there is high involvement of voice for employees, the direct decision-making process will have greater support from all stakeholders and the decisions will have a greater ability to include a variety of perceptions and perspectives to ensure that the outcomes are successful.

When an organization employs high involvement of voice from all stakeholders, there is a greater opportunity that decisions and actions of the organization will result in increased profits based on the decision outcomes.

Organizations view profit in different ways. A corporation may view profits as the income after expenses from the sale of goods and services. A school may assess profit based on the academic and social success of the students. Governments may assess profit through a lens of success of programs and initiatives that better support the wants and needs of the citizens. The key is the involvement of employee voice, the great access the employee has to share and receive information that helps to shape decisions, the greater the willingness of the employees to work together toward those established goals. For schools, the teachers having a greater voice in how instructional practices or behavior criteria will be used in the classroom creates greater willingness of the teachers to follow through with these practices. Similarly, in businesses, the input of the employees and the valuing of their contributions creates a greater willingness to work toward the business goals.

Creating an organizational environment that values direct interest and uses the value of voice of employees to further refine the interest of all stakeholders builds an operating system that helps to ensure the success of the organization. It is the increased involvement of voice and the valuing of varied opinions that will allow for the best possible plans and best possible resolutions. Many times, organizations fail to offer employees direct interest and the ability to share in the leadership process. When organizations have low involvement of voice, the repercussions cause harm to the systems. When an employee feels isolated and feels that they have a lack of input, the effects cause an erosion of the climate and culture of the organization. Moral drops and employees feel their efforts are not valued or having any impact to help the organization.

Low involvement of voice causes a spiral in the environment of the organization. Employee engagement in the process and the outcomes wanes because they feel that they are not valued or important. Their voice is not valued. Employees do not seek to improve themselves or work to grow their practice because they feel that nothing, they do will have a positive impact. As employee's interest falls, so also does the profits of the organization. Outcomes fail to meet expectations. This spiral does not have to happen. It does not have to be the reality of an organization or a school. If leadership values employee voice and engages them in a shared leadership process to address issues and goals, the organization can flourish. Valuing the voice of employees can seem like a daunting proposition. Many organizations have hundreds or thousands of employees serving in many different roles. How does leadership gain access to the voices of all these stakeholders? The solution is in the systems created.

Engaging employee voice in large organizations requires a systematic approach to accessing feedback. The process must be tiered to allow feedback in multiple means. Organizations have layers of leaders, some direct leaders are positioned within the organization hierarchy, and some of the indirect leaders are within the employee groups. Accessing these informal and formal leaders to help build engagement and allow for open feedback and discussion is a critical component to ensuring success in the shared leadership process. Understanding the impact of shared leadership on team function and the power of employee voice is an important leadership learning. Examining team effectiveness and the dynamic among stakeholders allows leader to direct the team to help support success in the decision-making process. Building team systems that allow the team to function efficiently requires the leader to develop team processes, such as intragroup conflict and consensus-building and emergent states, such as trust, cohesion and satisfaction, will contribute to our understanding of the effects of shared leadership on teams and their performance (Bergman, et al, 2012).

Intragroup conflicts hinge on the social-emotional tensions created when employee stakeholders struggle through the incompatibility, they experience from another employee stakeholder. The leader must work with the employees to develop trust and a willingness to learn from the other employee and build agreement on how they will work together. Another intragroup conflict is task disagreement. Not just in the process to complete the task but also in the agreed-upon outcomes of the tasks. How does completing the tasks support meeting the established goals? The leader needs to address these conflicts and keep the employee stakeholders focused on the agreed-upon goals and outcomes. Process can vary and giving employee freedom to work through process allows them to have greater ownership and drive to see successful outcomes.

Many times, employee stakeholders misunderstand the behaviors and actions of other team members. The very behaviors that shared leadership and valuing voice create as positive behaviors can be viewed as personal attacks. The critical lens and challenging the ideas shared by stakeholders can seem as a criticism of the work and ideas of other employee stakeholders. The leader has to commit to the team and the shared process. The leader has to ensure that all employee stakeholders feel that their voice is valued and that the ideas shared are discussed with equity and purposefulness. It must be repeated that not all ideas or plans of action will be accepted as the collective team idea or plan. Stakeholders must understand that just because they shared their idea does not mean that the team will agree with that idea. There is a give and take within the team dynamic which allows the best ideas to surface and the less-desirable ideas to wane. By limiting these misrepresentation moments, the leader can reduce the intragroup conflicts and keep the employee stakeholders focused on the goals and outcomes being developed by the team.

The more the employee stakeholders participate in leading the work of the team, the more varied the team members experience different types of leadership styles. The leader needs to manage the actions of the employee stakeholders and build consensus among the members. The ability to value voice and offer each stakeholder the opportunity to share and direct discussion will sharpen the end action plan that will be developed. In the shared leadership process, there is a need for more than one type of leader. To better serve the work of the team and reduce conflicts among members, it is prudent to have more than one type of leadership style. Leaders will need to define the roles and responsibilities for employee stakeholders serving on the team. This will reduce conflict and increase the employee value of voice because each member will know the other members roles and expertise.

To resolve goal conflict among the employee stakeholders, leaders will need to have the team focus on the vision and the mission. What challenges have been identified that the team is working to solve. The employee stakeholders must return to the original purpose of creating the team and why they have been positioned to work to solve these issues. As more of the employees use their voice and assume leadership, the need to resolve goal conflicts will reduce. The employees will gain a greater understanding of the issues and the problems they have been charged to address. Employee conflict is inevitable when you are grouping a wide cross section of people with a variety of perspectives. Managing these conflict moments can be reduced by opening the leadership roles to more of the team members and ensuring each voice is valued and important to the overall success of the team.

When leaders share leadership with stakeholders and during the shared process value voice, they need to understand that there is significant responsibility. Each stakeholder must embrace the collective responsibility to honor each voice and to demonstrate genuine respect for their teammates and the process. This responsibility is the foundation of the shared culture of the organization. There is also a responsibility to protect the dissenting voice, the voice that does not agree and does not want to follow the path. The true impact of a shared leadership process and a valuing voice is the development of a dynamic foundation of understanding and a culture that embraces each stakeholder for being unique and in the possession of different strengths and experiences. Through this true impact, the organization can develop a symbiotic and supportive environment that will allow for the creation of agreed-upon action plans and meeting goal expectations.

Employees have a duty of loyalty, duty to act in good faith and duty to account. When an individual is hired by a principal or a company, they are expected to only perform actions that will benefit the organization. Employees are required to obey, inform and protect all information that relates to the

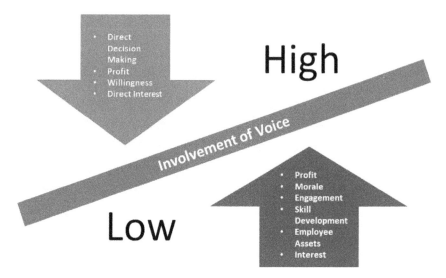

**Figure 6** The see-saw involvement of voice.

firm and its business operations. This situation prohibits employees from acting in their own self-interests. As a result, the duty of loyalty creates a legal contract between the individual and company in order to share a combined goal instead of competing interests.

An example of duty of loyalty would involve the directors and officers that are employed by large corporations. Directors and officers have a large number of duties and responsibilities within a company. The directors and officers are able to act as agents and make decisions for the firm. This situation makes it possible for both groups to make decisions that are only beneficial to them instead of the entire organization. Directors and officers have duty of loyalty in fiduciary matters. When the fiduciary duty of loyalty is violated, the directors and officers have become involved in self-dealing.

Next, employees must have a duty to act in good faith. When completing the task or assignment, the employee is expected to use the instructions provided by the principal. This situation provides an operational framework for the employee to complete the task while eliminating any self-dealing or competing interest. If an employee fails to follow the instructions provided by the firm, then the individual is in breach of duty and did not act in good faith.

There are three tests for determining whether diversification into a new business is likely to build shareholder value. The three tests are the industry attractiveness test, the cost-of-entry test and the better-off test. The first test is the industry attractiveness test. In order for a company to successfully diversify and to build shareholder value, the new industry must provide a strong opportunity for increased growth and revenue. The diversification into a new business must increase or at least equal the existing profits of the company's current investment strategy. The main goal of diversification is for a company to expand its market share into new related or unrelated markets. In order to be successful, the diversification must focus on the company's core competencies and goals.

The diversification into a new market must make strategic sense. Since all businesses are created to make profits for their shareholders, all business activities associated with the businesses must work toward increasing the return on investment. The more attractive an industry appears, the greater potential there is for a company to increase its profits. Attractive markets provide a greater market opportunity for diversification to investors and allow them to increase their return on investment and to expand their business operation. If a market appears unattractive, there will be no chance for increased revenue. Instead, shareholders would lose money in the diversification and the company would experience a loss in profits.

The second test that is used to determine whether diversification into a new business is likely to build shareholder value is the cost-of-entry test. Most companies will choose to diversify into a new business because the market appears attractive. However, an attractive market does not always provide shareholders with increased value. While the industry may be attractive and offer the potential for growth, it also opens the door for other competitors to also enter the market.

The more competitors that enter the market, the greater the level of competition will become. The cost for competing in the new market against several competitors will increase causing a decrease in profits. Second, a company could lose profits by heavily investing in entrance barriers for new companies. Entrance barriers would need to be implemented to make the market unattractive for potential new entrants. Third, if a company wanted to diversify into a new business by acquiring another company, it would need to make sure that the long-term profits would be greater than the initial purchase price.

The cost-of-entry into a new business must always provide a revenue stream that will be greater than the associated entry cost. If the initial cost is higher than the potential return on investment, the diversification into a new business is not feasible and should be avoided. A company's decision to diversify into a new business must prove to be more profitable for its investors than if the company were to only remain in its current market. If there is not a direct financial gain to the company, the shareholders will begin losing money at the entrance into the new business market.

The third and final test that is used to determine whether diversification into a new business is likely to build shareholder value is the better-off test.

This means that in order for a company to diversify into a new business, both the new and existing business would benefit from being under the same enterprise. When both businesses perform better due to being under the same parent company, they experience a joint synergy.

Synergy allows both companies to benefit from a new competitive advantage be developing a new business network. The supply chain and distribution channels also grow and experience a competitive advantage by working together. The joined companies also experience greater economies of scale by selling more products and reducing the amount of risk over a larger market segment. In order for the requirements of the better-off test to be met, both companies must experience a greater sum value of revenue and profits than either would have earned individually. Both companies must perform better under the same umbrella than they ever would have operated individually.

In order to build shareholder value, diversification must meet all three of these criteria. If only one or two of the tests are met, diversification may prove to be a poor choice for company. While the market may appear attractive and profits seem certain, this situation may only prove effective in the short term. Shareholder value must grow over the long-term business operation. In order for this strategy to be accomplished, the company must be attracted to the new industry. Second, the cost-of-entry and securing market share must be reasonable. Finally, both companies must experience a greater benefit together than performing individually. When these three tests are satisfied, diversification will lead to increased shareholder value.

Value relies heavily on listening to individuals and organizational communication. There are different types of listening that can be used to improve the listening skills of an individual. Next, listening is a crucial element of the communication process. Listening is required by an individual in order to understand the verbal and nonverbal meaning of the sender's message. While hearing the message acknowledges the message was received, listening ensures that the content of the message was fully understood by the receiver. As a result, listening is used to help identify the sounds and tone of a specific message so its content is properly received in the manner it was originally distributed by the sender.

The first type of listening is passive listening. Next, passive listening requires that the listening act as a sponge in order to soak up and absorb as much information from the sender as possible. Finally, passive listening requires the receiver to maintain the information that is provided to them without attempting to process its contents or enhance the data. As a result, the recipient of the message relies on passive listening when information is required to be shared but not modified.

The second type of listening is attentive listening. Attentive listening arises when the receiver expresses an actual interest in the content of the message provided by the sender. The receiver of the message becomes aware of the importance of the information contained in the message from the sender. This situation enables the receiver to miss actual information from the speaker by attempting to fill in the blanks of the content of the message based on their own personal attributes and assumption of what they want to hear.

The final type of listening is active or empathetic listening. Active or empathetic listening is considered to be the most effective and powerful form of communication in the negotiation process. Next, active or empathetic listening requires a large amount of effort for the listener in order to understand and interpret the message of the sender. Third, the listener uses active listening to hear the message as well as provide feedback to the sender regarding the initial message. This situation helps to improve the content of the original message and to establish a common ground between the sender and the receiver. Finally, both the sender and the receiver are able to limit the bargaining range of the negotiation process.

How information is communicated, perceived and then heard will determine will drive the form of power used by a leader. Therefore, it is important for us to be concerned about the different forms of power employed by leaders. A leader must understand the use and consequences of the five bases of power. A leader must understand what bases of power are the most appropriate and influential in a particular situation. The different forms of power will establish the level of authority in the organizational hierarchy. Power is used to determine a positive or a negative outcome within an organization, based on the leader's ability to influence the group members to achieve a goal.

First, leaders will need to understand coercive power. Coercive power is important in an organization because it establishes the consequences and punishments for the failure to complete a task within an organization. Leaders will utilize coercive power in order to ensure that each employee is motivated to perform at the expected level. This strategy will ensure that each employee understands the consequences and penalties of their actions if they do not comply with the organization. The second form of power that a leader will use is reward. Reward power is a tool used by leaders to motivate employees by providing rewards for a high level of performance. Leaders can choose to reward employees with promotions, bonuses, profit sharing, stock options and raises when a specific goal or objective is achieved.

The third type of power is legitimate. This type of power is assigned to an individual based on the position he or she holds within an organization. The greater the leadership position, the more authority the individual will have over the other employees in the hierarchy. Fourth, leaders will need to utilize referent power. Referent power is established when the leader is trusted and has earned the respect of the other members of the organization. Referent power is gained by a leader when the group or followers trust the leader to manage a situation.

The fifth type of power is expert. Expert power is used when a leader relies on their own knowledge, skills and abilities based on past experiences. As the leader gains more experience, their knowledge base will increase. This situation will cause the followers to gain more faith and trust in the leader's capabilities in order to meet the goals of the entire group. It is important for leaders to understand the different forms of power so they can use the right source based on the needs and requirements of the situation. It is very important to understand the differences among the bases of power and to apply the right leadership components to properly motivate employees. Finally, leaders must remember that power is perceived by the individual traits and intentions of their actions instead of a title or formal position of power. Leaders who implement the right bases of power will become more engaged in the business process and provide effective leadership in order to obtain a goal or an objective.

There are several factors that may serve as leadership substitutes. As a result, there are many different events and situations that will create a conceptual domain for the substitutes of leadership. The first domain is the professional orientation of the individual within the organizational structure. Professional orientation enables employees to have horizontal relationships in order to move up within the hierarchy of the organization. Next, the level of methodologically invariant tasks will be determined by the level and use of mass production and standardization. Methodologically invariant tasks not only focus on the end product but also the management and control process used to complete the task.

The third factor that may serve as leadership substitutes is performance feedback. Performance feedback will encourage an employee to achieve higher results and to gain a stronger belief in them instead of relying on a leader. The fourth factor is that the push/pull of the work will intrinsically motivate an employee to complete the task. When an employee is directly invested in a task, the intrinsic value of achieving the goal will increase, causing a pull of work. Fifth, cohesive and interdependent workgroups will act as a substitute for leadership. As a result, the individual will receive peer feedback on their performance.

The final factor that may serve as leadership substitutes is written goals, rules, guidelines and procedures; they will work to keep order within an organization instead of the need for a former leader. Written goals, rules, guidelines and procedures provide an impersonal form of communication that clearly state the expectations and eliminate the need for a formal leader in the organization. A substitute is an individual, place or thing that acts in place of an authoritative figure and is able to provide the same amount of leadership within an organization.

However, organizations must be careful not to replace substitutes with neutralizers. Instead of providing leadership, neutralizers will paralyze the workflow and cause the organization to become ineffective in its business process. Unlike substitutes that provide a benefit to organizations, neutralizers make it impossible for long-term relationships to be formed and cause a breakdown in the relationship between the employee and the task. Finally, neutralizers act as an "influence vacuum" that causes spatial distance between individuals and goal achievement. As a result, the rewards of the organization are not under the leader's control, and the employees become indifferent to the outcome.

The main purpose of an organization is to create value to gain customers and to increase its market share. Organizations are created when there is a desire or a need for a product or a service. The value or service is developed to provide both expected and perceived value to the consumer to improve their quality of life. The value that organizations create is determined by the current market share and the future needs of the consumer.

Organizations create value in many different ways. First, organizations must develop a value-creation system. A value-creation system uses the raw materials, knowledge or inputs to transform them into an output. The organizational value is determined at the input stage so attractive goods and services can be produced for consumers. The organizational environment also works to create value for the company. Organizations must utilize its human capital along with innovative technology for the conversion stage of inputs into finalized outputs. Once the organization has efficiently created outputs, the company must use the revenue to create additional products and services for new consumer needs.

The creation of value within an organization must be consistently analyzed and determined to meet the new demands of the consumer. To create value, organizations must use their resources in new and innovative ways to create new value. Creating new value is necessary to differentiate their organization from the competitors. Developing new value allows the organization to enter into new market and segments. In today's global economy, it is critical to be able to offer products to different market segments to gain consumer loyalty and increase market share.

Second, organizations must create more value. More value can be created by offering additional real and perceived value and expectations of the products or the services. The goal of creating more value is to persuade or convince the consumer that they will receive a better-quality product or service for their monetary investment. It is important for the buyer or consumer to feel that the good or service offered by the organization is enhancing their quality of life. Organizations can create more value by offering additional services or product features.

Third, organizations need to create a better value. Better value is established when an organization is able to build upon and expand on its existing value to consumers. The level of quality of goods and services the organization provides increases. When the quality of product or service is increased, consumers will recognize the increased value that was added. The better value will help to distinguish the organization's outputs from its competitors. Most organizations combine labor, raw materials and technology to create value to their outputs. The organization's specific skills are applied to satisfy the needs of consumers.

Entrepreneurs play an important role in value-creation process. The entrepreneur's main role in the value-creation process is to understand new needs of the consumers and to develop new opportunities for the organization. Once the new opportunities have been identified, the entrepreneur will then develop a new process for the organization to produce the new goods or services for the consumer. The entrepreneur will also gather all of the necessary resources to change inputs into valued outputs to increase revenue and market share.

The entrepreneur also develops a new efficient and effective business process by making sure the organization dedicates the proper number of resources to the new good or service. The entrepreneur also assumes the responsibility of any financial, psychological and social risk to the organization. The main function of an entrepreneur in the value-creation process is to manage and direct the new change to the organization to increase revenue, market share and economic growth.

The entrepreneur is also responsible for motivating the organization to develop new creative products or services. Next, entrepreneurs are responsible for focusing on the future need of the business to continue to compete in the global market. They are willing to assume the risk of new business models and strategies. By trying different strategies, entrepreneurs remain flexible and are able to implement new business processes quickly. The entrepreneur is responsible for increasing the value of the stakeholder's investment in the organization.

Finally, entrepreneurs are involved in the value-creation process by continually finding a new and improved way of satisfying consumer demand by making the organizations products and services more attractive than the competition. Entrepreneurs are extremely important to organizations and the value-creation process. Next, entrepreneurs help to create new innovation in products and services. Finally, entrepreneurs create new jobs and resources for the organization that enables them to continue to grow and expand into new markets around the world.

Similar to how entrepreneurs learn to lead the way with new products, inventions or ideas, organizational learning allows top management to make decisions in order to constantly improve and enhance the effectiveness of the company. Next, organizational learning improves the ability of top management to manage and guide the organization. Top management also has the ability to learn and control the complex business environment in order to use the organization's core competencies to make better programmed and nonprogrammed decisions. Organizational learning enables companies to explore new structures and to exploit strengths and weaknesses in order to make improvements.

There are four levels of organizational learning. The first level of organizational learning is individual. During the individual level, top management permits employees to learn and experiment using organizational resources. This strategy allows employees to gain more individual knowledge so they can contribute more to the needs of the organization. The individual level challenges employees and also provides them the opportunity to cross-train and to perform more duties and tasks for the re-engineering of the organization. The second level of organizational learning is group. The group level promotes collaboration and synergy with the use of cross-functional teams. Knowledge is easily shared between the different teams, and communication is improved throughout the organization.

The third level is organizational. The organizational level focuses on establishing the right structure and culture for an organization. In order for knowledge and communication to become a core competency, the organization must provide the correct atmosphere that promotes growth and development. For tall or mechanistic structures, an inert culture that encourages conservatism and low risk-taking will be necessary to maintain a shared vision. For flat or organic structures, an adaptive culture would be used in order to encourage risk-taking for growth and innovation based on its employees. The final level of organizational learning is interorganizational. The interorganizational level enables organizations to copy or imitate each other's core competencies. This situation will help to develop a normal business process within the business environment.

Managers can promote the development of organizational learning by acting at various levels in the organization. Within each of the four levels of organizational development, managers encourage knowledge and learning management of each employee. Managers also enforce the norms, duties, skills, values, culture and expectations of the organization. This strategy enables managers to develop each employee with specific skills and to increase the core competency of the organization. Managers will develop organizational learning by utilizing cross-functional teams and groups to solve internal and external problems within the company. Finally, managers can promote the development of organizational learning by acting at various levels to develop a cultural structure or framework that incorporates each employee into the mission and vision of the organization. As a result, managers will design an information system that develops a standardized business process and will improve the technical capabilities of the organization.

Within a school culture how stakeholders act and what they believe are important behaviors that will either propel a school forward into continuous improvement or it will stagnate and force the collapse of the school culture. The shared belief of the stakeholder obligations to behavior and quality of work will be a factor in the continued success of the school. There is an obligation of loyalty and truth in action in the school organization and to be a positive member of the team. To create an environment where loyalty is honored and acted upon, the leader must model these characteristics and teach stakeholders what the school culture values. Unfortunately, there are members of a school community that may not behave with a sense of loyalty to the organization or the stakeholders. Their actions may undermine the work of the stakeholders and the leader. The breakdown in the behavior of the stakeholder who is acting in a manner that does not value loyalty most likely is because of prior experiences. The stakeholder has had their behavior reinforced by negative interactions within the school system. The real failure is not that the stakeholder acts without loyalty, but that the leader caused or allowed this to happen.

The stakeholder is reacting to the conditions and the feedback that they experienced during interactions that were negative or situations where they experienced events where they were not protected or supported. Leaders either by their actions or by their inactions have either caused or allowed these negative interactions for the stakeholder. It is a conditioned response to the negative events they experienced. Leaders must take an active role in creating an environment where there is loyalty and that the stakeholder is protected from the harsh actions of other members of the school community. If the leader can create an environment where they have modeled loyalty and through their actions have demonstrated loyalty, then the stakeholders in the school will begin to act with the shared expectation of loyalty. It is through loyalty that the stakeholders will develop trust. It is through trust that stakeholders will take risks, and through risk, the shared voice and unique lens of each stakeholder will have true value.

It is the responsibility of each stakeholder to embrace the beliefs of loyalty and truth. When employee voice is valued, it is a function of the collective stakeholder behavior of loyalty and truth. The leader can set conditions for loyalty and truth, but the employees must internalize these characteristics and demonstrate a genuine belief in the value of voice. The stakeholders themselves as employees of the school and stewards of the culture must take the responsibility to act with honor and truth. It is through loyalty that employees will engage in shared leadership and value voice. Employee voice ensures that there is diversity of perspectives that are respected by all members of the team. As leaders engage employees in the energetic discussions that will support the work of the team, they must be careful not to alienate one stakeholder in favor of another. The challenge that leaders face is to make sure that each stakeholder is given space to share and in that process of sharing, there is value and respect. The team behavior of interactions and the valuing of employee voice must be a central focus of the leaders work with the stakeholders. As the team builds not only its formal culture but also its informal culture, the leader is the key member that can ensure that each stakeholder is not only told that they are valued but the team beliefs demonstrate and reinforce the true value of each employee and their voice as well. By building a culture of true valuing of employee voice, the team operational progress will be reflective of each member. If stakeholders believe that employee voice is not important or is not a valued part of the work of the team, they will begin to distance themselves from the work of the team. The employees will feel that their lens is no longer important. That the shared experiences they have endured and the outcomes they have worked to enact have little importance would be detrimental to employee voice.

If, however, employees feel that the struggles they have gone through and the solutions they have worked to implement are important. That the lens they have because of their experiences is an important part of the valuing of employee voice and that voice is critical to the success of the team, then the stakeholders will put in the effort and time to make sure the team meets its goals. Employees need to believe that they are an important part of the ability for the school to be engaged in continuous growth and improvement. The culture of the school cannot improve, cannot change to meet the greater needs of the stakeholders, or cannot address real needs for change unless employee voice is authentically valued.

The valuing of employee voice will be the foundation of the culture of change. The ability for employees to feel that they are important and are trusted by the leaders will become the energy for cultural improvement. The actions of the leader regarding valuing employee voice and cultivating an environment where the diverse perspectives of the employees become an important step in developing a culture of shared leadership and valuing voice. If the actions of the leader do not demonstrate a genuine belief in the value of employee voice, the employees will not trust the leader. They will not risk engaging in the shared leadership process or put forth the effort to work for change. The actions of the leader can undermine any good intentions that the stakeholders might have toward working to achieve the stated goals.

## Reference

Bergan, J. Z., Rentsch, J. R., Small, E. E., Davenport, S. W. & Bergman, S. M. (2012, Jan-Feb). The shared leadership process in decision-making teams. *The Journal of Social Psychology*, *152*(1), 17–42. https://doi: 10.1080/00224545.2010.538763. PMID: 22308759.

# Chapter 6

# THE POWER OF WORKER VOICE

The worker voice is different than the focus on employee voice. Worker voice refers to the member of the team that is serving in a subordinate role to the current team leader. Ensuring that there is value to each member's voice and creating consensus of action and outcomes is not only the role of the leader but also each worker within the team dynamic. Developing agreement of task performance, the best alternatives to the current system and evaluating outcomes are achieved by giving power to the worker voice. The very team members who put in the time to collaborate build understanding and agreement to help solve the challenges to meet a goal. By creating this environment of agreement, the stakeholders are not searching for the correct answer as much as they are working toward consensus of purpose and action. The foundation of shared decision-making is building agreement among the workers on the team while still valuing their voice in the process. The worker stakeholders have to share their experiences and knowledge of the topic and offer their unique perspectives, and from the ensuing discussions consensus will be achieved on the best action plan moving forward.

It should be noted that consensus does not guarantee quality in the decision-making process, or the effectiveness of the action plan developed by the stakeholders; it does mean that the team did, through discussion, create an agreed-upon action plan. By valuing the worker voice on the team, the consensus developed allows the stakeholders to believe that their final decisions are ones that will best serve the organization. The role of the worker voice and the shared process of leadership ensures that consensus will be developed when planning outcomes and actions. The valuing of the worker voice helps define the shared vision and the overall strategies the team will use to develop solutions to the identified issues of the organization. The more the workers are leading and sharing in the process, the greater understanding they will have of the outcomes and the greater their sense of ownership will be.

The interactions of the stakeholders within the team create the operational foundation of the team dynamic. Workers collaborative problem-solving with the leaders create a clear mission for the team and the organization. Valuing worker voice suggests that when more team mem- bers are involved in the leadership of the team, members are more likely to understand the reasons for the solution and be committed to its implemen- tation (Bergman, et al, 2012). It would be expected that shared leadership and valuing worker voice and input would be related to increased consen- sus among team stakeholders. Creating a team environment where worker voice is valued, the team members assume that the shared leadership role should help the team to develop operational trust among the stakeholders. Trusting worker voice happens through repeated discussions and problem- solving within the team, where team members demonstrate that they can be trusted through their actions and discussion exchanges. There is a willing- ness to share leadership and responsibility, there by indicating to the other stakeholders that they can be trusted.

From this development of trust and the collective shared worker voice, the team can move toward developing their mission. Team responsibilities and roles that will protect worker voice energize the team to act upon its mission. Participating in the shared development of the team mission also develops trust among the stakeholders. That shared trust allows the workers on the team to feel comfortable in sharing their expertise and perspectives as the team works on resolving challenges and developing action plans to address the organizational goals. Building a culture that values worker voice sends a message to the stakeholders that leadership honors and respects the varied voices shared within the team and has confidence in the collective abilities of the workers to lead the team to successful outcomes. Valuing worker voice sends the message that leadership trusts the stakeholders and that the leaders can be trusted to include the workers in the decision-making process. Once trust is established, the team can enact the mission to develop and refine the operational vision of the organization. The vision will set the long-range goals that the stakeholders will be engaging in to develop plans and expectations for the organization.

The valuing of the worker voice and the development of collective trust among team members can be eroded if team members try to usurp other stakeholders and attempt to take control of the team and its actions. It is assumed that all worker members of the team would like to assume some leadership roles during the teams work because they have invested in the work of the team and the vision developed by the team. If the team dynamic is that worker stakeholders will have opportunities to lead and there is a collaborative process established among the team members, there is an increased likelihood that the shared leadership process will increase trust among team members and allow efficiency in enacting the vision developed by the stakeholders.

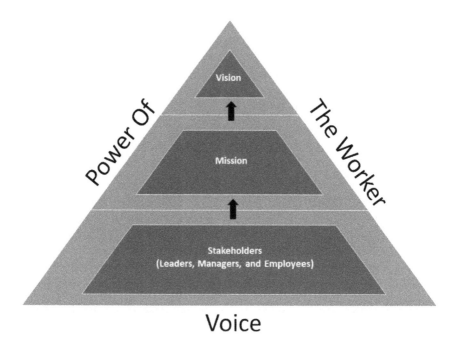

**Figure 7**  The pyramid of making voice work.

There are various stakeholders within an organization. Each group of stakeholders will have different interests and expectation based on the performance of the company. The first group of stakeholders is capital market stakeholders. Capital market stakeholders are shareholders of an organization that provide a large source of capital and funds for the company. The second group of stakeholders within a company is product market stakeholders. Product market stakeholders include the primary customers that purchase goods and services from the firm. Next, suppliers are considered product market stakeholders. Suppliers are concerned about the success and strategic competitiveness of the company based on its ability to generate and guarantee the highest level of return on investment. A supplier will want to form a partnership with a company that is able to sell the highest amount of goods and services to customers to create economies of scale and scope. The final product market stakeholders are host communities and unions. Host communities form an agreement among the different entities in order to increase revenue and sustainability. Unions are stakeholders who are concerned with the needs of the employees such as employment, wages and safety.

The final group of stakeholders is organizational stakeholders. Organizational stakeholders include employees, managers and nonmanagers.

Organizational stakeholders primarily focus on the internal network of individuals who make up the framework of the organizations. Employees are a stakeholder in an organization since they have a direct investment in the success of the firm. The more successful the firm is able to become, the greater the reward the employee will receive. Next, managers are considered stakeholders since they are rewarded based on the profitability of the firm. Finally, nonmanagers provide the knowledge and skills required by the firm to gain a strategic competitive advantage.

Within organizations, different groups and stakeholders will compete for scarce resources which will cause a high level of conflict. It is the ability of one stakeholder group to overcome the other groups within the organization in order to achieve their objectives and goals. Organizational power is used to resolve conflict. However, if organizational power is not used correctly, it can be easily be abused and cause the organization to become ineffective. The ability to properly designate and assign resources to support the entire organizational structure is determined by what group or individual that holds the organizational power.

It is important to maintain a balance of power between different groups of organizational stakeholders. A balance of power is important in order to manage the politics within an organization. Organizational politics occur when different departments or stakeholders compete for the same quantity of scarce resources. While they can have a negative connotation, politics should be used to make the best argument to use resources that will increase the core competencies of the organization. This situation will help an organization to keep a checks and balances system to make sure that resources and organizational power are correctly applied for the entire organization.

Maintaining a balance of power will also enable the organization to manage the politics in an organization and to experience the advantage of properly utilizing its resources. With a balance of power, the organization will not suffer from groupthink by individuals who only share one point of view and who discourage creativity or innovation. Next, a balance of power will help to establish a clear level of authority within the organizational hierarchy. Resources will be given to the department or functions that can produce the most value or high-quality outputs for the benefit of the entire organization. The control of information will also improve with the balance of power since the organization will be able to analyze and tailor the collected data to meet the needs of the different divisions within its hierarchy.

If there is no balance of power between the different groups of organizational stakeholders, one group will become more powerful and will dominate the decision-making of the company. Any opposing or dissenting views will be ignored. This situation would cause an organization to become inert and to not experience any new innovation or creativity. Next, a lack of balance of power would cause more conflict and dissention within the organization.

Managers and employees would become dissatisfied. As a result, the effectiveness of the organization would decline, causing it to become stagnant in the business environment. A balance of power will help to ensure that the best interests of the organization are always considered with the use of politics and the support of each group of stakeholders. There is a difference between the efficiency effect and the replacement effect. The efficiency effect compares and analyzes the results of a monopolist to two competitors who are part of a duopoly. Next, the efficiency effect then compares the benefit of the duopolistic firm to one that is not located in the industry and does not earn a profit. As a result, the efficiency effect makes the incentive of a monopolist to produce new innovation opportunity stronger than new or potential entrants into the market. The monopolist will develop a higher level of risk and will have more to lose when new entrants enter the market. New entrants will cause the price point of the outputs to decline. This situation will cause a drop in revenue and market share for the monopolist firm.

While a monopolist would have the ability to innovate, it would have a lower level of motivation than a firm that exists in a competitive economic environment. When there is a drastic new innovation opportunity, a firm in a competitive economic market would be more willing to focus on producing innovation in order to gain a competitive advantage. The failure of one firm to innovate will enable another firm to develop new innovative opportunities. This situation will cause firms in a competitive market to aggressively compete for market share by developing new products in order to retain consumer loyalty and market share.

The efficiency effect and the replacement effect could operate at the same time. When there is competition between established firms and new entrants to develop new innovation opportunities, three effects will concurrently operate together. The three effects include the efficiency effect, replacement effect and sunk cost effect. The effect that will control the firms in the market will be based on the current economic conditions of the market. When new entrants possess a low chance of producing new innovation opportunities, sunk costs and the replacement effect will be the guiding factors for the business strategy. The monopolist would use its current capital in order to develop innovation opportunities to keep enacting high entrance barriers for potential competitors.

However, the efficiency effect will be preferred when the monopolist fails to develop new innovative opportunities. This situation would enable new entrants to produce new innovations and to gain market share from the existing firms. New entrants will need to gain a quick competitive advantage in order to efficiently and effectively compete in the existing market. Competitors will consistently be looking for new ways to improve core competencies and economies of scale through innovation. Finally, the replacement effect will dominate when there is no real threat for new innovative opportunities to develop from outside of the industry or economic market.

The expectations regarding the relationship between leader reward and punishment behaviors and group cohesiveness, drive and productivity are based on two basic assumptions. The functioning group is defined by four criteria that include two or more people who interact with each other or influence each other's behavior, share a common goal and see themselves as a group. The group consisted of a supervisor and the group members to be in the same area.

The examination analyzed the actual level of interaction between the leader and group members and the level of inclusion and safety each member felt. In order for each individual to feel that he or she was a member of a particular group, two conditions had to be met. First, the close vicinity of the group members among each other would lead to a high level of interaction. Second, the inquiries that were linked to the group processes were based upon the description and response of each individual who reported to the same leader. This assumption helped to analyze the workflow and the level of independence between the leader and each of the group members.

If rewards and punishments are rewarded individually to members within a group, the entire group will become dysfunctional when the workflow is interdependently linked and will become ineffective. In order to maintain an effective group, leaders will not want to reward and punish only certain individuals. Instead, it is better for the leader to keep the group intact and reward and issue punishments to the entire group, based on the effectiveness. Finally, leaders will not want to use noncontingent factors in order to impact the perception of the group.

There are expectations regarding the relationship between leader reward and punishment behaviors and group cohesiveness, drive and productivity. The leader reward and punishment behaviors will be positive or negative based on the perception of efficiency and effectiveness of the entire group. This stronger the relationship between the leader and the group, the more cohesive the group will become. Group drive will also be influenced by the leader's reward and punishment behaviors. The drive of the group will also be directly linked to the variables and productivity with the use of the non-contingent reward and punishment system.

Finally, the leader reward and punishment behaviors will have a direct relationship with productivity. There is an important connection between the relationships between the perception of a leader's subordinates and the leader reward and punishment behaviors. Contingent behavior of rewards and punishment is positively related to group cohesiveness, drive and organizational effectiveness. While incentive plans can work to influence group members, the right form of reward and punishment behavior needs to be implemented. If a leader uses the wrong form of reward and punishment behavior, then that person will lose trust and legitimate power by the entire group.

It is important to focus on followers in our study of leaders and the leadership process. When this situation occurs, it becomes difficult for an organization to provide effective leadership. The organization will want to encourage leaders to form a strong relationship with each group of followers in order to develop an efficient leadership perception process. When leaders focus on the followers, they can make better inferences and gain the ability to understand and adapt to meet the needs of each follower.

Based on the leader's focus on the followers, they can use the automatic inferential process to develop a causal link based on the culture of the environment and the amount of control needed over each employee. Second, leadership can rely on their focus of followers to use a controlled inferential process that allows the leader to better understand the different actions for a desired outcome for an organization. Third, recognition-based perceptions allow a leader to use preexisting knowledge of leadership in a particular context or situation. When the leader focuses on the followers, the leader is able to understand a larger cultural background and potential variables in order to better understand the situation and to make a more effective decision.

The focus on followers in the leadership process will allow an organization to understand how and where followers would fit into the effectiveness of a leader incorporating Hofstede's cultural dimensions in the Leader-Member Exchange model. The first cultural dimension is collectivism and individualism. Collectivism is the organizational belief that the group of followers should receive top priority. The followers believe that their own values, beliefs and needs should come before anything else. Individualism occurs when a follower focuses on his or her own level of success and achievement within an organization. An effective leader will need to understand the dynamic and to create an environment that develops recognition and a reward-based system in order to form a strong "in-group" of followers.

Next, leaders must focus on the followers to determine the perceived level of power distance. The higher level of power distance within an organization, the followers will perceive that leadership will focus on the recognition-based process to achieve results. Third, leaders must determine the perception of masculinity and femininity within the organization. Masculinity is the amount of assertiveness used to gain material possessions while femininity focuses on establishing long-term relationships. Effective leadership depends on focusing on the followers to determine what approach will work best to motivate them and to create a positive perception of headship.

Fourth, the amount of uncertainty avoidance will help to determine the acceptable level or perceived level of authority. When there is high uncertainty avoidance, followers will not utilize the inference-based process. However, the followers will adopt the recognition-based process in order to earn recognition and rewards for their individual productivity. The final cultural dimension is fatalism or locus of control. In order to provide effective leadership, a leader must communicate the responsibility of each follower in a situation. With high fatalism, followers will perceive that the actions of the organization are out of their control. However, a high level of locus of control puts the responsibility of an action on the follower and analyzes their individual impact on the overall outcome. The combined use of these cultural dimensions will determine how and where each follower fits into the organization and leadership process based on a cross-cultural perspective.

How organizational power is shared is a critical component to the valuing of worker voice. On any team, there are members who will be assigned tasks and given responsibilities that will help the team be successful. Workers serve a subordinate role on the team. They are to follow the direction and path established by the leader. That does not mean that the voice of the worker is not important. It just means that power within a school is not equal. The principal serves at a different power level than the teaching staff. The collective worker voice of the teachers is incredibly important and skillful leaders will use the worker voice to help them to grow understanding and insight to issues impacting the school. In many ways, the worker voice is more influential than the leader's voice. Workers will tend to listen and respond to fellow workers where they may have apprehension to listen to the leader. There is separation of power due to role responsibilities and that can breed mistrust. However, if worker voice is celebrated and honored for its importance, then the leader can capitalize on the collective wisdom of the workers. The worker is the stakeholder most connected to the conditions and culture of the school.

Impactful school leaders will understand how each worker fits into the organizational system. How each worker has a unique lens that filters what they see and how they react. It is incumbent upon the leader to understand the unique dynamics of the team and to engage the workers in discussions that not only ask for their feedback but also celebrate their willingness to share. It is the worker voice that will eventually share an organization's true beliefs and culture.

## Reference

Bergman, J., Rentsch, J., Engal Small, E., & Davenport, S. (2012), The shared leadership process in decision making teams. *The Journal of Social Psychology*.

# Chapter 7

# DEVELOPING SHARED LEADERSHIP CULTURE

There is a disconnect between the perceived and actual value of shared leadership on impacting change in an organization, especially in schools where there are inherent systemic blocks to true shared leadership and shared information. Schools tend to silo information; by doing this, they block the ability to use collective wisdom effectively. This is not because the stakeholders do not want to engage in shared leadership or valuing voice; it has more to do with the lack of training and resources to support this cultural shift. When asked, teachers and staff want to know what is happening, they want to know the decision process and they want to be involved in the decisions that will impact their work. Without this understanding, the organization or school cannot move to a true shared leadership model. There is a disconnect between the layers of stakeholders. In top-down design models, leaders will identify an issue, address that issue with a plan and then inform the stakeholders of the plan for implementation. There is little collaboration or sharing of viewpoints and experiences. There is no exchange of ideas that can bring about the best solution to address an issue; in short, the leader actions lack a shared lens and do not value voice.

In the enacting of plans, there is a push for implementation from the leader at the bottom to the stakeholders above. The agenda and action steps are pushed up and forced upon the stakeholders. Leaders prop up the process to ensure that there is compliance, not buy-in or ownership by the stakeholders. This process is doomed to fail. The forced action plan builds resentment and frustration among the stakeholders. When the plan fails, the stakeholders see this as a self-fulfilling prophecy. They knew it would not work, but the leaders did not have a mechanism for stakeholders to share their experiences or expertise. The leader's actions and choice of leadership style will have a tremendous impact on the climate of the culture in schools. The alienation of the staff, the disregard for the needs of students all in the process of completing an agenda will eventually cause the cultural environment to collapse. The

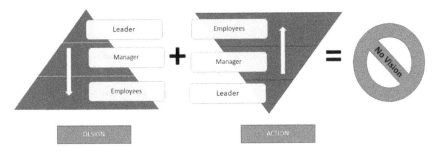

**Figure 8** The singular "me" culture.

leader will lose authority because the stakeholders will not trust the decisions of the leader.

The conventional wisdom of shared leadership is that as stakeholders interact within the process, they develop situational relationships that connect each stakeholder to the team and to each other. In developing a shared leadership culture, there are specific tasks and roles for both the leaders and the stakeholders. There is a development of norms and values that happens when stakeholders who have a set agenda of goals, work collectively to meet these goals. These relationships contribute to the team members style of interaction and types of socialization. Members who are embedded in shared leadership generally are more committed to the team process and its values and norms. If the team dynamic that is created values shared leadership and the valuing of voice, then the team will share the power and responsibilities associated with the expectations of the team goals and develop trust.

It has been argued that the potential for dysfunctional political maneuvering increases when power is controlled by one dominant individual (Bergman, et al, 2012). As the team develops its culture and begins to test each other's strengths and weaknesses, there is a natural ebb and flow to the stakeholder interactions. These interactions will have a significant impact on the culture and how each stakeholder feels about each other and the team. The leader has the responsibility to help stakeholders work through these challenges and move to a more collaborative exchange as part of their working dynamic. Using effective shared leadership methodologies and working collaboratively with the stakeholders, the eventual outcome of team culture should create a bond among the members that is based on trust and value. Working to this point in a team dynamic takes time and effort.

How team members share power and how they work to value voice of each member will be central to how the culture develops to ensure efficiency and effectiveness. The ability to share power and leadership while focusing on the outcomes will help to develop a cohesive culture among stakeholders. By sharing leadership and valuing voice of each stakeholder, the culture of the team will develop authentically and naturally. This culture of value and shared power will make the team far more effective than if led by a single individual. Teams that developed cultures that embraced shared leadership and valuing of voice showed to exhibit more trust and connectiveness. It is because of the developed relationships that the stakeholders created through interactions and time. How the leader creates an environment that embraces and supports these types of collective behaviors among the stakeholders will allow a culture to flourish where team members get alone with each other, stick together and stay focused on their assigned tasks and develop positive relationships that allow for disagreement and discussion that drive innovation and creativity.

Stakeholder satisfaction of the team culture and the interactions among each team member is an important aspect of developing a successful, shared leadership culture. The satisfaction the stakeholders feel is a result of the experiences they shared as part of the team. Team culture is a process that must be cultivated and continue to be worked through all the different interactions and work of the stakeholders. Team culture in shared leadership and valuing voice is a continuous improvement process. If the leader and the stakeholders do not commit to continually working on culture, tensions and misunderstandings will begin to erode the threads of connection developed over time. All the team efforts will dissolve, and the team will begin to exhibit dysfunctional behaviors that are toxic to the effective functioning of the team. The role of the leader is to manage the interactions of the stakeholders through this management the leader can influence the effectiveness of the team.

The shared leadership process will allow for the development of a positive team culture that has team interactions and social connections that support the collaborative work of the members. It is the social connections that are developed and cultivated through the strengthening of the stakeholder relationships that facilitates effective interactions of the team and its work toward its goals. As members continue to take opportunities to lead within the shared structure of the team, there is an increasing sense of accountability for the success to meet expectations and goals. This culture of accountability and shared responsibility to meet expectations and goals ensures that stakeholders feel an increased commitment to the team and its goals. A culture of positive relationships and equitable interactions allows the stakeholders to have an increase sense of responsibility not just for the meeting of the established goals but also to support each other during the decision-making process. This sense of mutual accountability is essential to developing a culture that functions in such a way that will support the free expression of ideas, including the sharing of dissenting opinions that will force a greater dynamic of conversations that will yield better outcomes.

In a shared leadership culture, there is greater support for all the stakeholders as well as the leader. In a shared leadership culture, members believe that their member stakeholders are more invested in the success of the team and are also more agreeable to the outcome decisions that the team makes. How the leader interacts with the stakeholders is also important to how the members feel about being part of the team and how they are valued for their voice and perspectives. The leader has to build avenues for stakeholders to assume leadership roles during the workings of the team. It is the leader's job to ensure that stakeholders are engaged and satisfied with the process and progress of the team. A culture of shared leadership and valuing of voice has a direct relationship with the amount of satisfaction stakeholders feel about the team and the work that the team has accomplished.

Shared leadership culture is reliant on the skillfulness of how the leader's behaviors help to foster the conditions of the working environment that will celebrate the voice of each stakeholder. The leader's action has a direct relation to the effective or ineffective performance of all stakeholders. The ability of the leader to be able to connect meaningfully with each stakeholder, to be a support to the efforts of the stakeholder and to manage the team dynamics has proven to be a significant factor in how well the shared leadership culture is ingrained in the operating actions of the team. It is evident that the leader is significant in the development of a meaningful culture, and it is also evident that each stakeholder has an impact on the development of the shared leadership culture. How stakeholders value each other, how they interact with one another and how they share ideas, information and expertise is critical for the development of an inclusive culture. Stakeholders' interactions have a great impact on how other team members view their role on the team and how others are contributing to the overall success of their endeavors.

The significance of developing a culture that has buy-in from the stakeholders is essential for team success. Cultures that value each stakeholder and give importance to the efforts and experiences of other members have a power effect on how each member views their connection to the team. Additionally, the influence of the leader is central to how well the team operates and how successful the team will be in meeting the established goals. These are all essential aspects to building culture that will allow each stakeholder to have voice and their perspectives will be valued and discussed as part of the process to develop criteria for successful decision-making. When the leaders or the stakeholders act in a fashion that causes others to question the intentions of the stakeholders can have a profound negative impact on the work of the team. Trust would be eroded because stakeholders will feel that they have been made to feel that their work and their voice are not valued or that the leader does not believe that their contributions have any value for the team.

The value of voice is important in all companies, organizations and forms of businesses. In the first type of business, we see voice is within a sole proprietorship. A sole proprietorship is considered the most simple and common form of business entity. The structure of a sole proprietorship is unstructured. Next, a sole proprietorship is easy to establish and terminate based on the desire of the individual. A sole proprietorship is operated by the individual who is considered the owner. The owner is entitled to all of the earnings and profits of the sole proprietorship. However, the owner is also responsible for all liabilities and debts that are incurred by the sole proprietorship.

In order to form a sole proprietorship, an individual must file with the state and government in order to obtain a business license. The business license permits the owner to do business within the state under a trade name or "Doing Business As" (DBA) name. Sole proprietorships are taxed as based on the individual and not as a separate legal entity. In order to report the earnings and losses, the owner must file a Schedule C and estimated taxes form for self-employment.

There are many advantages of a sole proprietorship form of business. First, a sole proprietorship is easy and inexpensive to create. Since the sole proprietorship is the easiest form of business to form, there is a minimal business structure. The cost of operation remains low. Next, a sole proprietorship allows the individual to be the owner of the business and to have full control of the business operation. Every decision that is made involving the business is made by the owner. Third, the owner of a sole proprietorship has the advantage of retaining all of the profits earned from the business. Finally, a sole proprietorship is easier to file tax information than other forms of businesses. The tax rate is also lowest for the sole proprietorship form of business.

However, there are also several disadvantages of a sole proprietorship form of business. First, a sole proprietorship has unlimited liability for the owner. Since the owner is responsible for the business, there is no separation of liability or obligations. The owner of a sole proprietorship risks both his business and personal assets in the event of debt. Next, raising money to operate a sole proprietorship can be difficult. The funds used to operate the business will be used on the owner's ability to generate or borrow money. The funding is limited to the individual's funds or through bank loans. As a result, the burden of ensuring the success of a sole proprietorship is the responsibility of the owner.

There needs to be a relationship established between the landlord and the tenant of a building where the business operates, whether it be a small business, an organization, a government facility or a school. A landlord is the lessor of the building. The tenant is referred to as the lessee. Based on the relationship, the tenant takes temporary custody of the portion of the building or property through a lease. The property being leased is called the leasehold estate. The lease is the legal document that binds the landlord and the tenant into a contract for the temporary ownership of the land.

The landlord–tenant agreement also requires that the tenant must pay rent for the space being utilized for the specified amount of time of the lease. In order to establish a landlord–tenant agreement, there are certain elements that are required for the existence of a landlord–tenant relationship. First, any landlord–tenant relationship that last over one year must list the names of the landlord and tenant(s). Listing the names of the individuals involved in the lease will provide clear guidance to who is responsible for the lease and ownership of the land.

Second, a landlord–tenant relationship is required to detail any implied or expressed intent to create the landlord–tenant relationship. Since the landlord–tenant relationship is a binding contract, both parties must agree to the terms when entering into the contract in order for it to be considered legal by the courts. Third, a landlord–tenant relationship is responsible for describing the property being leased by the landlord to the tenant. Fourth, the time or length of the lease must be clearly stated in the landlord–tenant relationship. The length of the lease will be used to state how long the tenant must remain and what the penalties are if the lease is broken. The final element required for the existence of a landlord–tenant relationship is the amount of money a tenant is required to pay as rent to the landlord during the term of the lease.

The leadership relationship contributes to a good execution of strategy. Good strategy and good execution are critical to having good management. In order there to be good management within a company, there must be a strategy to follow. The strategy is based on the core values of the company and acts as the map as to where the company is heading in the future. Once the strategy has been established, it needs to be correctly executed. All business decisions that are made need to be defined and centered on the strategy. Good management can be seen when the strategy is executed correctly.

Strategy and execution are the "core" functions of the management structure. The better the company's strategy and its execution of the strategy, the more financially successful and profitable it will become. Good management of a strategy will give a company a sustained competitive advantage over its competition. If a company does not have a good strategy or it is poorly executed, the company will suffer and will lose its advantage and not be able to compete in their current market. Good management allows a company to strategically advance into new markets while minimizing any potential risk to the organization.

There are six strategically relevant components of a company's macroenvironment. The components are political factors, economic conditions in the company's general environment, sociocultural forces, technological factors, environmental factors and legal and regulatory factors. Together, these six components work together to determine how the company operates and what outside factors would impact its business operation. It is important to analyze them together with the use of a PESTEL analysis to see how they affect the company and its buyers, suppliers, substitute products, rivals and new entrants into the industry.

The first factor is political. Political factors deal with the stability, operation and interaction of the company with the government where they are operating in. If a company is operating in more than one country, it will need to make sure to understand the acceptable level of social policies and expectations in each country. Trade regulations will also be a factor. The number of imports, exports and costs associated with them will need to be determined. Finally, the tax policies will also need to be established. A company will need to make sure to fully understand the impact of all political factors so they do not get penalized by the government for what could be perceived as inappropriate business practices.

The second factor deals with economics in the company's general environment. The components the company will want to pay close attention to are the value of money, exchange rate, interest rates and inflation. The investments the company makes and the level of disposable income will depend heavily on value of money. The higher the level of inflation or interest rates, the more costly it will be for the company to expand its business operation. The company will also want to pay close attention to the unemployment rate, credit level and amount of disposable income of its target market. When the unemployment rate is high, the amount of disposable income drops dramatically causing a decrease in spending. This situation causes a decreased return on investment for the company.

The third factor is sociocultural. Sociocultural factors deal with the population and demographics of a company's market segment. Key factors that a company will need to focus on are the age, culture, diversity and values of their target market segment. The level of income and wealth is also important to determine. Depending on the population, the level of disposable income will vary given the age and diversity of the consumers. Education and lifestyle would also need to be analyzed. In demographic areas with a higher level of education, the quality of life is greater, which means the company will want to offer higher end products.

The fourth factor is technology. Technology is an important factor that changes rapidly in today's business market. It is important for a company to choose the newest technologies that will help it to gain and sustain a competitive advantage. Technology is also a large business expense and the technology platform the company chooses should be carefully analyzed in order to make sure that it the best investment and will not become obsolete in the near future.

The fifth factor deals with the natural environment of the company. Depending on where the company operates, environmental laws will play an important factor. Waste disposal, carbon restrictions, air pollution, building restrictions, clean water usage, dumping and the consumer's attitude about the environment will need to be taken into consideration. Operating a company with business policies that help protect the environment can be costly and these expenses will need to be determined before business operations begin.

The sixth factor focuses on legal and regulatory issues. Health and safety regulations must be followed. Labor laws that include child labor, overtime, worker compensation, benefits and product regulations must also be followed. Failure to follow legal or regulatory guidelines would cause a business to incur large penalties or fines and could even be reason to lose their operating license. When operating in multiple countries, it is important to understand the legal regulations in each area. These six factors work together to help determined the macroenvironment of a business. It is important for manager to look at these factors and to conduct a PESTEL analysis. PESTEL stands for political, economic, social, technological, legal and environmental factors. The PESTEL analysis will allow manager to develop a strategic plan to help their company survive in the macroenvironment and to sustain a competitive advantage over its competitors.

The culture within an organization plays an important role to its success and execution of strategy. The corporate culture creates a unique personality and becomes the "DNA" of the company. Corporate cultures of organizations vary dramatically from organizations in different markets. As a result, culture operates both as an ally and obstacle to strategy execution within an organization. First, culture can contribute to the successful execution of a company's strategy. A strong culture will unite the employees under a single belief and corporate vision. When the culture is synchronous with the strategy, it will become an ally to the corporation. In order for the culture to be an ally, it is important that the company's core values and expectations are clearly communicated to every employee. When the culture is tied to the organization's mission, it will become a powerful tool in strategy execution.

There are three actions that are necessary for the culture to become an ally of a company's ability to execute strategy. The first action is to focus every employee's attention on the actions that are most critical to the strategy execution effort. When a company is able to motivate employees to work on the most critical actions, new innovative ideas and business processes are formed. As a result, the level of product defects decreases, and there is an increase in the quality of the organization's overall value chain. The more streamlined and focused the organization becomes, the better it is able to execute its corporate strategy. Corporate culture becomes an ally by concentrating all of the employees toward a single goal and strategy.

The second action that is necessary for culture to be an ally to strategy execution is that it can produce peer pressure for employees. Peer pressure will help to encourage and motivate employees in order to equally work alongside each other. The more unified the employees become, the greater level of strategic fit the company will experience. This situation promotes the execution of strategy by developing a sense of loyalty and comradery among the employees. The employees within the company become united behind the goals of the organization. As a result, the organization's core competencies and capabilities are increased and the strategy is able to be accurately executed.

The third action that is necessary to make culture an ally is to be successful in energizing employees and to make them committed to the strategy of the organization. Culture can be used to empower and direct employee efforts toward achieving the goals of the company. When the employees are more focused, the level of productivity will improve causing an increased return on investment. Employees will continue to become more energized by their previous success. The employees within an organization will continue to set new benchmarks of quality and production helping the company to better execute its strategy.

Culture can also act as an obstacle to the execution of strategy within an organization. If the attitudes and behaviors of the employees within an organization are cohesive, the culture will become a huge obstacle to executing strategy. If the employees are not in "harmony," additional time and energy will be wasted trying to accomplish objectives and goals. Next, if the culture is not in sync with the strategic vision, the organization will not be able to be successful in its strategy. If there is not a direct relationship between the culture and strategy, the organization will be operating with employees who are self-dealing leading to the prevention of the execution of strategy.

Next, culture can weaken the business processes and framework of an organization. An unhealthy culture within an organization can deter the efforts of managers and leaders. When the behaviors of employees do not support the vision of the company, objectives and goals cannot be completed. As a result, the company is unable to properly manage its employees and execute its strategy.

Culture is a very important element in the success of executing strategy. The culture within an organization needs to empower its employees. The more empowerment the employees experience, the tighter the fit occurs between the culture and the execution of strategy. Culture is necessary to improve the attitude of the organization. With the implementation of a strong corporate culture, employees will become invested and will work together as a team. Culture can be an ally in increasing productivity and the efforts of all employees. Finally, culture must be routed in the core beliefs of the organization. This strategy will allow the culture to be conducive to promoting new innovative ideas, synchronizing employee and corporate beliefs, and executing strategy.

There is a difference between the general environment and the industry culture/environment. The general environment is divided into seven specific categories or segments that include demographic, economic, political/legal, sociocultural, technological, global and physical. The first segment involves demographics. The demographics of the general environment will determine the population and age of the various individuals. Next, the demographic segment will analyze the income and geographic distribution of the population. Finally, demographics are used to determine the ethnic mix so companies can understand the amount of diversity in the market segment.

The second segment is economic. The second factor deals with economics in the company's general environment. Organizations will want to pay close attention to the value of money, exchange rate, interest rates and inflation. The investments the company makes and the level of disposable income will depend heavily on value of money. The higher the level of inflation or interest rates, the more costly it will be for the company to expand its business operation in the general environment. Firms will also want to pay close attention to the unemployment rate, credit level and amount of disposable income of its target market. When the unemployment rate is high, the amount of disposable income drops dramatically causing a decrease in spending. This situation causes a decreased return on investment for the company which will change the status of the general economy.

The third segment is political and legal. The political and legal environments should be determined to be stable and able to sustain future business in the new market. The higher the amount of instability, the harder it becomes for a company to gain entry into a new market. Next, the legal environment will impact the selection of an entrance mode. The legal environment will dictate the number of imports, exports, tariffs and quotas the nation will allow. A firm will need to understand the expectations and restrictions placed on trade and direct foreign investment.

The fourth segment is sociocultural. Sociocultural factors deal with the population and demographics of a company's market segment. Key factors that a company will need to focus on are the age, culture, diversity and values of their target market segment. The level of income and wealth is also important to determine. Depending on the population, the level of disposable income will vary given the age and diversity of the consumers. Education and lifestyle would also need to be analyzed. In demographic areas with a higher the level of education, the quality of life is greater which means the company will want to offer higher end products.

The fifth segment is technological. Technology is an important factor that changes rapidly in today's business market. It is important for a company to choose the newest technologies that will help it to gain and sustain a competitive advantage. Technology is also a large business expense and the technology platform the company chooses should be carefully analyzed in order to make sure that it is the best investment and will not become obsolete in the near future.

The sixth segment is global. The global segment focuses on important political events that occur within the general environment. The development of new industrial countries will be used to determine the attributes and diversity of the institutional attributes. The final segment is the physical environment. Companies that operate in the general environment must understand the energy consumption and sources around the world. This strategy will enable a company to operate more efficiently and to reduce its cost structure. Next, the firm will be able to reduce its carbon footprint and to help promote a green environment. Finally, the physical environment is important to help protect the natural resources and raw materials of each nation for future generations of consumers.

The industry environment is a set of factors that directly impacts and influences a firm's strategic competitiveness. A firm will be forced to make decisions and take actions based on the impact of the factors in the industry environment. In order to gain a competitive advantage, an organization must use its core resources to develop a strategic management process that will increase its market share. Next, companies will need to be able to defend themselves from the potentially hazardous factors in the environment to compete against other firms. The first main factor in the industry environment is the threat of new entrants. New rivals into an existing market will be a threat if it is easy for them to enter into the market without any barriers.

The second factor is the bargaining power of suppliers. The more power the suppliers have in the market, the more they control the pricing and cost for the business. The third factor is the bargaining power of buyers. The power of the buyers is determined by the economy. If the economy is good, and there is a lot of product selection for the buyer, all of the purchasing power becomes controlled by the consumer instead of the company. This would make it difficult to set prices or to predict a steady return on investment. Next, the threat of substitute products will impact the sustainability of a firm. Finally, the intensity of rivalry among competitors will determine the sustainability of a firm within a particular market segment. As a result, the higher the intensity of the rivalry among competitors will determine the amount of competition between existing companies and new entrants attempting to enter the market.

While every firm has a culture, not all cultures are relevant for a decision-maker or analyst. Under certain conditions, it is important to pay attention to culture within an organization. In most organizations, culture is directly linked to the performance. The culture affects the performance measures of a firm. The culture of a firm will be used to influence the behavior of each employee when making a decision.

Decisions-makers within an organization should not perform an action that would cause a conflict with the achievement of organizational values and goals. In some instances, a decision-maker or analyst will ignore the culture of a firm in order to pursue a course of action that would benefit themselves instead of the entire firm. However, some firms have an unethical culture. This situation will cause an employee to choose the appropriate course of action to meet the goals of the firm. If the goals are unrealistic, the employee may be encouraged by the organization's culture to lie or cheat for goal achievement. An individual with a high moral code would choose to ignore the influence of culture in order to make the proper decision based on his or her beliefs.

Next, it is important for decision-makers or analyst to pay attention to culture when there is no formal authority. When there is no formal authority, the level of control is minimal. This situation enables a firm to experience a loss of control and structure. In order for a decision-maker or analyst to make a decision, they will need to be able to establish personal relationships within the firm. Since there is no formal culture, an informal culture will need to be implemented to gain support and understanding for the action.

Finally, decision-makers and analysts must analyze culture when there is conflict with the business process and strategy of the firm. When each member of a firm shares the same values and ideas, a strong structure and organizational culture is created. This situation will enable the firm to gain a competitive advantage and to operate more efficiently and effectively. However, a firm that does not have a unified culture will experience diseconomies of scale, scope and a lack of learned economies. When a firm within an industry shares a common culture, culture will not be used as a resource to increase or decrease competition or market share. Decision-makers and analysts will be able to ignore the influence of culture. In industries where there are multiple cultures within firms, the impact of culture will become more relevant for decision-makers and analyst.

Understanding the culture and relationship between leaders and groups is important. One of the main duties of a leader is to influence and motivate their group of followers. The LMX is based upon the characteristics and traits of the leader and the level of trust perceived by the group. In order to build a strong relationship with a group of followers, the leader will need to demonstrate to the group their own level of commitment to the success of the group in achieving a goal.

First, a leader must use cooperation as a function of leadership. Leaders must use the psychological forces that determine the variables and complexity of the environment. In addition, leaders must learn to self-sacrifice for the greater need and benefit of the entire group. Each group member's perception of the leader's willingness and ability to self-sacrifice will improve the level of trust and communication.

The understanding between the relationship of leaders and groups in organizations needs to focus on the characteristics and traits, as well as the implemented leadership styles based on the self-sacrifice and different bases of power. Leaders must be trained more effectively in how they can clearly communicate their vision and the objectives that they personally value to achieve a goal. This situation will enable the leader to demonstrate and develop a perception of self-sacrifice to the entire collective or group. The amount of trust in the leader from the group will help to link the self-sacrifices of a leader to the cooperation of the followers.

In order to improve the perception of the relationship between a leader and the group, trust and the identification of expectations are important to use cooperation as a function. Next, there is an independent relationship between identification and trust. Trust can be developed from the perception of the group members of the leader. Trust could also be formed as a result of identification of independent effects of the different variables. As a result, trust and identification are an important component of an effective leadership process.

Finally, the relationship between leaders and groups is important to understand because it is crucial to effective leadership. Leaders must understand the group dynamic in order to implement the right form of leadership. Groups can require either transformational or charismatic leadership based on the particular situation and need of the complex environment. Understanding the relationship between leaders and groups will help to develop goal-setting and expectations required to achieve an organizational objective.

The more understanding there is between the leaders and the groups, the more motivated and invested the individuals become. Every individual will move beyond their personal self-interests and begin focusing on the collective needs of the group. As a result, the workflow process improves. The LMX will also improve, resulting in an increase in organizational effectiveness. Leadership needs to be based on self-sacrifice to eliminate the desire for personal gain so everyone can improve the value and success of the entire group. Individuals will become more invested and will gain a greater level of identification and trust, enabling the leader to increase the function of cooperation to improve the leadership process.

Culture is important in aiding the understanding of the meaning behind certain actions and events of individuals and organizations. There is logic and a pattern to the decision-making process of an individual or aleader. The culture of a leader in an organization will be determined by the history or influence the individual has had between the group members and factors in the environment. Each individual has their own understanding of what is considered right or wrong, based on their cultural background. Cultural influence exists in the mind of every leader and employee. Depending on the individual and organization, culture will determine the attitudes and norms within the internal and external environments. It will also help to establish the roles and expectations of each member in the organization. Culture is a mental process that enables the individual to understand the different cultural dimensions and their individual interactions with a leader and the leadership process.

Leaders must understand the cross-cultural perspective and perception in order to provide successful leadership to a diverse workforce. In today's global environment, leaders must interact with individuals from various backgrounds and cultures. This situation will cause the leader to operate in a multicultural environment. Leaders that incorporate a cross-cultural perspective will be able to establish cultural and incorporate the "ethnicity" of each employee.

In order to understand leadership, leaders must understand the different cultural dimensions. Leaders must also utilize its perception in order to make cultural inferences to create a successful leadership process. When the leader and group member are from the same cultural background, an automatic inferential process occurs. The automatic inferential process is based on the close proximity and general understanding of the outcome during an event. However, leaders can form perceptions using the controlled inferential process. The controlled inferential process uses a more analytical approach to determining the outcome of an event. Instead of relying on a general assumption, this strategy analyzes all possible causal agents and then chooses the best course of action for the desired outcome of the organization.

Leadership relies on an individual's ability to use recognition-based perception. Recognition-based perception allows a leader to use previous or established knowledge about a similar event in order to make a decision about a current action in the organizational environment. Finally, culture should play an important role in aiding our understanding of leadership. Culture allows a leader to better understand the background and thought process of each follower. As a result, leadership can use a cross-cultural perspective in order to create guidelines that utilize the strengths of each culture. This strategy will enable leaders to make the organization more effective and to gain a stronger competitive advantage in the global business market.

There are different ways that the informal organization and the norms and values of its culture affect the shape of the organization. First, organizations can use the informal organization to help support the formal structure within the organization. While organizations may have a hierarchy of control, they will still need to form contingency plans on how to deal with potential issues or problems. The informal organization defines the culture and social structure within the company.

The link between the formal and informal organization is important to a company because it creates unity between each department and division within the hierarchy. In order for the informal organization to succeed, it must utilize the norms and values of the defined culture. The norms and values are used to set the tone and to standardize the internal behavior. When the norms and behavior are standardized, the organization becomes a cohesive unit. The chain of command will also be reduced to a minimum number of levels with the use of values and norms. Combining the norms and culture with the formal structure of the organization will influence each employee on how to act and what is expected. Planning, development and the improved establishment of new goods and services will also increase due to the determined norms and values within the organization.

The informal organization will help the organization to maintain a firm structure, while allowing for flexibility in the changing environment. With the use of informal norms and values, the organization can gain more control. As a result, organizations can become more effective with fewer levels in the overall hierarchy. Tall organizations with many bureaucratic processes can be eliminated while producing a greater level of output in less time. As the organization grows, it will no longer have to rely on a large number of managers to function. Instead, the organization will be able to utilize a structure with a reduced number of levels. This strategy will prove effective because it will eliminate additional time and steps to finish the process.

As the organization grows, the informal organization will help to keep the company flexible so it can adapt to the new environment. The informal organization will also help to improve the design of the company. The culture and norms will guide the structure of the different processes and activities needed to achieve the stated goals and objectives. Finally, the informal organization will allow a company to develop contingency plans and adapt its business operation to meet the needs of the consumer and the ever-increasing complex environment. There is a relationship between the size of the organization and its ability to effectively manage each component. The informal structure within an organization will help to provide the missing connection between the formal leadership and the internal needs of the company.

The origin of organizational culture is based on the founding philosophy of the organization in order to increase its effectiveness and productivity. Organizational culture is based on the values of organization in order to determine and guide the actions of every employee for the desired outcome. Terminal and instrumental values are used in order to achieve the anticipated outcome and to establish the appropriate mode of behavior in the organization. Organizational culture is also important for communicating the norms and acceptable behaviors in the organizational structure.

The origin of organizational culture is based on four main sources that include the characteristics of people within the organization, organizational ethics, property rights and organizational structure. First, the characteristics of the people are the main source or the organization's culture. The values and norms of the chief executive officer and top management team will determine the culture of the organization. Depending on the different values, every organization will have a unique culture. Organizations will need to make sure to attract and hire employees who share the same beliefs and values in order to maximize efficiency and productivity. The founder of the organization sets and determines the culture. Over time, the culture becomes more distinct, and new employees of the organization will learn to share the vision and mission of the founder.

The second source of origin for organizational culture is organizational ethics. Organizational ethics are important because they define personal beliefs of the founder and set the guidelines for all acceptable internal and external behavior and business practices. Organizational ethics are determined by the individual, professional and societal beliefs. In order for an organization to be successful, it must support and share the values of its stakeholders in order to form a strong business relationship with its environment. Organizational ethics are important because they dictate and control the behavior within a company.

The third source of origin for organizational culture is property rights. Property rights are the rights given to employees by an organization to use its resources. Property rights give each employee or stakeholder the right to develop different norms, attitude and values in the organization to achieve their goals. The distribution of the organization's property rights is a method to motivate employees. Based on the different property rights, employees will be able to become more integrated and invested in the organization through employee stock option plans, profit-sharing, bonuses and promotions.

The fourth source of origin for organizational culture is organizational structure. Organizational structure is a formal system created in order to assign control and responsibility of tasks to every employee within the company. Since each organization's structure is different, every organization will have a unique structure that incorporates its values, norms and beliefs. Organizational structure can be designed with a mechanistic or organic framework. An organizational structure that utilizes a mechanistic structure will encourage a stable and conservative culture. However, an organic structure will promote a culture that is liberal, highly innovative and always looking for new ideas and business processes to compete in the environment.

With the combination of the characteristics of people within the organization, organizational ethics, property rights and organizational structure, every organization will have a predetermined culture. However, every culture within an organization will be different. Like people, no two organizations are exactly the same. Each organization is unique, based on the beliefs and values of its founder. Depending on the focus and interaction of these four sources, the origin of organizational culture will be determined. The combined use of these four variables will set the culture of every organization apart from one another and will cause the norms, values and beliefs to become specialized to the needs of the particular business.

Newcomers learn the culture of an organization by indirectly observing the values, behaviors and actions of the existing top managers and employees. In order to learn the culture of an organization, newcomers are required to gather information about the different cultural values based on their own observation. However, this strategy can become dangerous if the newcomer chooses to observe an employee who does not believe or follow the expected culture of the organization.

The most successful way for a newcomer to learn the culture of an organization is through socialization and role orientation. Socialization will enable the newcomer to become immersed in the organization and to form relationships with every employee. Next, role orientation will help a newcomer to learn how to respond and react to a specific situation. Third, newcomers can learn the values and the culture of an organization through the stories, ceremonies and language of the organizational founders. Organizational stories, ceremonies and language are important ways for the company to communicate and enforce the norms and expectations to all newcomers.

Organizations can develop an institutionalized role and individual role orientation to encourage newcomers to conform to the stated norms, values and beliefs. There are several tactics that an organization can use to establish the orientation of institutionalized and individual roles. The first tactic organizations can use is collective tactics. Collective tactics provide the newcomer with a common learning environment so the newcomer can learn a standardized response to a situation. Individual tactics, the learning experience of each newcomer will be unique and focused on the particular current situation. Second, formal tactics separate the newcomers from the senior employees during the introduction phase into the organization. Once the formal tactics have been established, the newcomer will learn informal tactics by completing on-the-job training.

Third, organizations will use sequential and random tactics. Sequential tactics will give the newcomer detailed information on how and when organizational tasks will be completed. As the newcomer progresses through the ranks of the organization, they will learn additional duties. Random tactics enable the newcomer to gain knowledge based on the immediate need of the organization. Fourth, there are fixed and variable tactics. Fixed tactics establish a set timetable for each stage of the newcomer learning process. Variable tactics do not provide a specific timetable for the completion of tasks or processes.

Fifth, there are serial and disjunctive tactics. Serial tactics establish a mentor while disjunctive tactics require the newcomer to figure out and develop their own way to behave in the organization. Finally, organizations can use divestiture and investiture tactics. Organizations that use divestiture tactics provide neglect and have negative support to all newcomers until they learn on their own how to conform to the established norms. Investiture allows organizations to provide positive input and feedback to help newcomers gain support and acceptance.

In order to successfully integrate newcomers, organizations will need to use a combination of institutionalized and individual role orientation. The success of the implementation of newcomers into the culture of the organization relies on the commitment to ethics. Ethical behavior is critical in ensuring that the right newcomers are hired and used to improve the success of the organization through the desired business practices. Depending on the structure of the organization, the level of integration of the newcomer will vary to different degrees. In a mechanistic structure, organizations will want to use an institutionalized role to ensure that every newcomer goes through the same process. However, organizations with an organic structure will want to utilize an individualized role approach in order to enable the newcomer to implement their specific resources and talents to expand the business' culture.

When new ideas or customs are introduced to individuals, they can incorporate them into their current culture. The situation will cause the current culture to absorb the new values, traditions and physical aspects into the current culture. As a result, the current culture will begin to gradually change.

The customs, attitudes and values of the culture will grow and expand to include a more diverse view and understanding of the different people in the global economy.

In order for cultural diffusion to occur, both the physical environment and technology are necessary to influence the cultural change. The climate and topography of a nation will help to determine the natural barriers of the individuals and customs of the individuals. The type of food, clothing and other materialistic possessions of individuals of a culture are determined by the physical location of the nation. Next, technology is used to influence the material culture of a nation. Technology is used to determine the successfulness of a market segment and to help nations develop in order to support the manufacturing and production of outputs. Depending on the location of the nation, cultures will be unbalanced across the different nations based on the resources available.

International businesses should be sensitive to the charge of cultural imperialism. Cultural imperialism occurs when one culture dominates another in the same geographic area. Cultural imperialism can occur by the replacement of traditions, artifacts and a nation's remembrance of heroes. With a global economy, trade barriers are being removed and companies from different nations are able to gain access into new foreign markets. With the introduction of new products and traditions, existing cultures can be replaced by new products, ideas, policies or technologies.

With a potential charge of cultural imperialism, firms must be sensitive to the existing culture of a market. It is important for a company to be sensitive to the needs and existing cultural expectations of the community. While it is important for businesses to provide products and services that meet the current needs of the consumers, firms must also be careful to remain consistent with the existing culture and way of life of the market segment. Although innovation and changes are unavoidable in all cultures, companies should take steps and precautions to minimize the negative impact to the existing society and culture. In order to reduce the impact to the current culture, companies should seek the council of the nation's leaders in order to ensure a shared understanding between the business and nation. As a result, the company would be able to provide new products and services in a stable environment that would not replace the existing culture of a nation.

Organizational structure combined with culture is very important for a firm in order to gain a competitive advantage. Next, organizational structure is used to establish the formal and informal policies of a company. Formal organizational structure will establish the rules, regulations and hierarchy within the firm. An informal organizational structure will determine the social and cultural configuration of an organization.

Firms will need to determine the appropriate organizational structure base on the goods and services it provides to consumers in the markets. The two main types of organizational structure include functional and multidivisional. The basic business functions would include finance, human resources, manufacturing and production, marketing, operations, and research and development. This structure enables a firm to expand and increase the resources for each specific division when necessary.

The second type of organizational structure is multidivisional. A multidivisional structure is referred to as an M-Form. An M-Form structure groups the functions of a firm into single business units instead of functions. This strategy allows a company to focus on individual outputs and to design business functions specific to each output. The firm will be able to produce and market outputs independently of one another. As a result, the firm will be able to produce and market single business units in various geographical economic markets in the environment. A firm will gain a competitive advantage by being able to control and operate various single business units in different markets separately without increasing the amount of risk to the firm.

Next, organizational structure is determined by centralized and decentralized decision-making. Centralized decision-making is conducted in one location or corporate headquarters for the entire company. However, decentralized decision-making occurs within the different levels and locations of a company. When competing in an international economy, companies will need to allow international subsidies located in different countries to make independent decisions based on the requirements of the local consumers. Within every organization, there needs to be a balance of authority and control. The structure and level of control depends on the organization's goals and also the complexity of the environment. In an unstable environment, organizations will want to reduce the amount of risk and have a culture of centralized decision-making and standardization.

If the level of complexity is low and there is growth in the environment, organizations will want to encourage new decision-making by implementing decentralized decision-making and using mutual adjustment. The advantages of standardization and centralization are to promote stability and predictability in all business actions and functions. Centralization is best used in tough economic times when every decision is important to the company to reduce risk. Decentralization and mutual adjustment are important for an organization to create new and innovative products and to adapt to a new global environment. Finally, organizations operating in international or global markets will need to use both centralized and decentralized decision-making to properly customize the output for each region to maximize its return on investment.

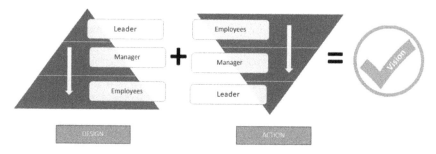

**Figure 9** The shared "we" culture.

School culture is based on the shared collective vision developed through the interactions of the three main stakeholders. If the students are the employees, and the managers are the teacher, and the principal serves as the leader. There is shared value and a collective process where each group member is responsible for the development and enacting of the school vision. It is equity of importance among all three stakeholder groups. The environmental conditions reinforce the belief that all three groups are equally responsible for developing and acting upon the shared vision. The more complex the school environment is, the more that each stakeholder group must be valued in the development of an interactive culture. It is through the school culture that the organization is going to create its collective vision and each stakeholder group must be recognized and heard during the sharing of information and the development of the mission and goals of the team.

Culture is one of the most difficult aspects of a school organization. Schools are dynamic institutions with a wide range of events and happenings that have an impact on the daily operation of the school. How leaders go about developing a shared culture and ensuring that each member is valued and important will aid in stabilizing the operational systems within the school. By having decisions that are driven by the actions and work of the stakeholders will help to develop a culture of inclusion and shared recognition and responsibility. As stakeholders engage in this type of improvement work, the culture of the school will change. Culture can change from internal forces such as the behaviors of one stakeholder group or a collection of behaviors that are counterproductive for the school. Culture can also change from external forces that are exerted on the school. Political or public demand will change the school culture. How do stakeholders operate in a system that lacks sustainability is an important question that leaders need to address if they want school culture to be a positive force in developing meaningful systems and practices that best serve the needs of students.

If leaders and stakeholders work together and the foundation of the design is the stakeholders (employees), then the ownership and buy-in will be easy. The stakeholders created the design, they had leadership and voice in the decision process and now they act on the plan they created. When action is driven from the stakeholders and supported by the leaders, there is a greater understanding and agreement. The stakeholders now embrace the work and want their efforts to yield success. To ensure that the stakeholders are collaboratively engaged in the leadership process and are embracing the diverse voice, it is important that they embark on training to develop these skills.

A school culture that is rooted in the collective wisdom and diversity of the stakeholders will be more proactive in addressing issues and quicker at developing solutions. Even though the shared leadership and valuing voice process takes more time than a top-down autocratic decision-making process, it will be quicker because there will be far less repeating of endeavors. Fixes that the teams create with a shared process will be better developed and more reflective of the issues, ensuring success. In the end, the longer work of creating action plans through a shared stakeholder process will create faster more lasting change that will feel less stressful for all stakeholders. Schools are notorious for resisting change. The staff of schools do not want to see change because they feel insecure about their role and how they will be assessed in completing their goals. Change brings another level of stress and strain on the school culture.

To combat this stress on the school culture, change needs to go through a shared leadership and valuing of voice collaborative team structure. The stakeholders on the team need to feel empowered to recommend change and to create the process to change. If the team can model this shared process when engaged in their work, then the stakeholders can embrace this model for all aspects of decisions that must be made to support the mission and vision of the school. Eventually, a new structure will develop creating a shared leadership process that values voice throughout the entire school.

## Reference

Bergman, J., Rentsch, J., Engal Small, E., & Davenport, S. (2012), The shared leadership process in decision making teams. *The Journal of Social Psychology*.

# Chapter 8

# KNOW, PLAN, ACT (KPA)
# THE GAP IN PROCESS

Addressing the action steps of a shared leadership team is an important aspect of evaluating if shared leadership and value of voice is authentically part of the team dynamic. Is shared leadership really part of the operating system of the team or is it something that has been discussed but not implemented? This evaluation process is important to know how well the shared leadership process and the valuing of voice has impacted the work of the team. Knowing what the stakeholders believe is shared leadership and valuing of voice is the first step in ensuring that these strategies become part of the team behavior. The leader and the stakeholders have to have a clear understanding of what it means to them to be part of a shared leadership team. How well each stakeholder assumes a leadership role during the work to meet the goals and expectations is a key measurement of how well shared leadership is accepted by the team.

Before any action can be taken by the leader to develop a shared leadership culture, the leader must first be reflective about their true beliefs. The positionality of their core value structure will determine what type of school culture is created. How does the leader truly feel about shared leaders and valuing voice? If the leader is being directed to, or forced to, enact a shared leadership model but does not agree with the principles of this style of leadership, then the school culture will be toxic and fail. Schools do not respond well to autocratic rationale-legal leadership that does not allow for the sharing of perspectives and experiences.

As leaders begin this process of changing culture, they need to decide what version of shared leadership do they value. Is it shared leadership among the chosen stakeholders or is it a shared leadership that embraces all stakeholders? Through a careful process of reflection and introspection leaders can determine what style of shared leadership they embrace. Now leaders need to teach it to their stakeholders. Stakeholders need to understand the conditions and expectations of how leadership will be shared and how voice will be honored and included. Once leaders have a clear understanding for themselves and have shared with stakeholders, then the school can begin the process of converting to a shared leadership model. The leader can create training and development opportunities so that stakeholders can learn about shared leadership and how to engage and embrace every voice.

Implementing a shared leadership process will take time. There will be significant learning that stakeholders will need to complete, and they will need to practice these skills. There will be a significant amount of practice needed in valuing voice. How to embrace diverse voice and lens and then use these statements to help develop agreement for the goals and the accompanying action plan. How to embrace failure and difficulties for the stakeholders, and how to develop trust and respect. These will be challenges that the leader can assist in helping stakeholders as they develop their skills in leadership and voice.

Once the leader has facilitated the professional development, stakeholder practice of the skills, and the collective stakeholder voice in gathering what needs to be addressed; then the real work can begin. The stakeholders are now prepared to embark on creating a culture of shared leadership and valuing voice. Leading the shared process and valuing voice will shift from the leader to the stakeholders, and they will begin to own the process and they will establish the value in sharing voice and leadership. This shift will now allow the real shared leadership and valuing voice.

What types of plans will the stakeholders develop in a shared leadership and valuing of voice process? The stakeholders will collectively develop a shared culture where the norms and values are reflective of the membership. The working dynamic among stakeholders is one where the work is as valuable as the outcomes. The work is an active endeavor meeting expectations of goals and living in the process of shared leadership and voice. The planning for action in this type of collective process far exceeds the traditional top-down model in quality of outcomes and stakeholder buy-in.

Building a plan of action for the team and creating a shared understanding of the steps that will be taken to support and protect the opportunity of each stakeholder are necessary to assume a leadership role. Each stakeholder should know the shared beliefs the team has regarding shared leadership and valuing voice. The leader holds a key role in ensuring that all members of the team know what the shared leadership values are for the team and what the expectations are for stakeholder interactions. Building clarity around the norms and values of the team and how shared leadership is important to their operating systems is how the leader can make sure that the team is functioning at its best.

The actions of the team, the systemic behaviors of stakeholders as they interact with each other and how they assume and release leadership to other members of the team are important factors. How the team members act when functioning as a team must be based on the shared beliefs that have been developed by the team stakeholders. The shared beliefs that the stakeholders know they have been a part of developing the framework for how they act within the team. It is these actions that will build connections and a sense of value among the stakeholders. In many ways, it is more important for how the stakeholders act with each other, than what they said was what they know about their beliefs. Their actions will make each stakeholder either feel that they are valued and important or that they are being dismissed as irrelevant to the leadership and decision-making processes.

When what is known cannot be expressed and shared because the organizational systems do not have a process for collaboration, then there is limited information being used for decisions. The greatest wealth of understanding and experience is with the employee stakeholders. In schools, this is especially true because teachers are constantly engaging and working with students. Their level of understanding and how they can contribute to the decision-making process are exceptional. The depth and breadth of understanding and experience can only produce outcomes that are doable and successful. The most successful cultural dynamics are where the stakeholders are driving the discovery, learning, sharing and acting. It is through these levels of teamwork that the best solutions emerge. By sharing the leadership and responsibilities, stakeholders can focus on the aspects that best suit them. Go to where their skills will be impactful and offer real change for improvement.

Where the information gap is in the process and who owns the information can impact the success of a school culture. If the leaders possess the information and did not engage the stakeholders, then they are the only ones who understand the gap and how to address it. If the leader shares the gap, what that gap means for the school and what the expectations are, then the stakeholders can collaborate and through shared and valued voice develop a solution can be developed. The challenge with information gaps or system gaps is that many times the stakeholders involved do not know that there are gaps. The issue at hand is that the leader must create a system that will first be open and share the body of information and the known gaps within the information. From this process of sharing, the leader can then activate a system of engagement that will connect the stakeholders with the shared information and stated goals. These planning processes that the leader engages will help to begin to build the structures that will become the culture of shared leadership and valuing voice. If the stakeholders can have access to the information and a system that will allow them to work collectively with a specific plan to achieve the stated goals, then the team will be able to meet the established expectations. The "know" process is one of the most important aspects of developing a shared leadership and valuing voice behavioral system. To have all stakeholders know what is known and to have access to what is not known is the first steps to engaging the team in its work. Too often the stakeholders within an organization do not know the relevant information, they are left out of the gathering process, and more importantly, they are left out of the decision-making process.

The planning process should be reflective of the stakeholders and the vision and mission. Planning to act becomes a key component of the process of engaging stakeholders in shared leadership. As stakeholders work toward goals, they need to be able to embrace diversity of voice. Planning to embrace variety of voice must be purposeful and meaningful. Leaders must have positionality of what they believe about valuing voice and shared leadership. What do they truly believe? What does the leader embrace and feel comfortable with as part of a shared leadership process? The leaders must decide if they believe in shared leadership and shared voice. If they do, then the leaders must plan to share their believes. Stakeholders will work best if they feel that they have been included in the most important information. Stakeholders also will function better as a team if they believe that the leader also believes in shared leadership and voice.

The leader must plan to first share but then to have a step-by-step training that teaches the stakeholders how to act within an operational system that embraces shared leadership and valuing voice. Once the stakeholders have gained understanding of how to act in a system of shared leadership, the team will need to plan how they will act within that team. The norms and values, the rules of discussion and engagement of experiences and expectations will all shape how the team accesses and uses shared leadership and valuing voice. Leaders are responsible for ensuring that the stakeholders understand and can act within the created system of shared leadership and voice.

Stakeholders working in a shared system then must create a plan to act. The idea of creating specific action steps that address the goals and expectations become central to the success of the team and the organization. In schools there is a tendency to act before planning. School staffs are great at addressing the cause of issues and because they experience the organizational conditions of these issues, they become solution-driven. It's not necessarily a bad lens to be solution-driven; the drawback is that the fixes created may not address the root causes of the issues. The critical step of "act" is one that needs to be developed through the shared process of inquiry, sharing voice and perspectives, as well as a shared development of action steps that address the goals and the issues that are impacting the school operating environment.

The benefit is that teachers by nature want to do what is in the best interest of the school and students. They want to see improvement, and they want the best operating system possible to support the students. To make sure that when the team moves forward to act, the steps that they will take will be developed using the most accurate and varied information from a variety of sources. Stakeholders can use this information as the basis of their collaborative shared voice process. Stakeholders can grapple with the gathered information to offer as much insight into the issue and eventually create action steps that all stakeholders can embrace and complete to help change the operating environment.

If leaders can access the stakeholders and gather information from their diverse lens, then the planning and action of the stakeholders will allow for better solutions and a better plan to act. If the model is top down and the leader has all the information and does not involve and engage the stakeholders, then any action plans that were developed will eventually become fixes that fail. The loop created only continues to protect information from the stakeholders and continues to create fixes that have no chance to address the issues or create lasting solutions. Who possesses the pertinent information and how this information is either shared or protected will determine how stakeholders interact and act to meet the stated goals? However, if the team of stakeholders are working collaboratively with a leader who is willing to share information and allow the stakeholders the opportunity to express their views and contextual understanding of the issue, there is a greater chance for the stakeholders to work through their differences and create a working operational plan. When teachers act, they will be acting on plans that were developed from the process of sharing information and sharing leadership.

One last challenge that leaders will need to address is the different levels of engagement of internal and external stakeholders. Internal stakeholders who operate within the behavioral system experience the difficulties and the issues. They experience the gaps in the operating system and can see that there are real needs to improve. They see the issues in a first-person lens because they have personal experiences. External stakeholders see issues with a much different lens. The perspective they have is one of informal and secondary experiences. The external stakeholders are invested in the organization's success, but they have not lived through the issues. They have operational knowledge and an understanding of how the internal stakeholders felt while working within the organization, but they do not have personal experiences. Leaders will need to engage both sets of stakeholders for their understanding and their resources. Leaderships will need to activate both sets of stakeholders, and through a shared leadership and valuing voice system ensure that all stakeholders have clarity of understanding of the conditions and the issues.

Administrative agencies within companies and organizations typically rely on informal rulemaking which is also known as notice-and-comment

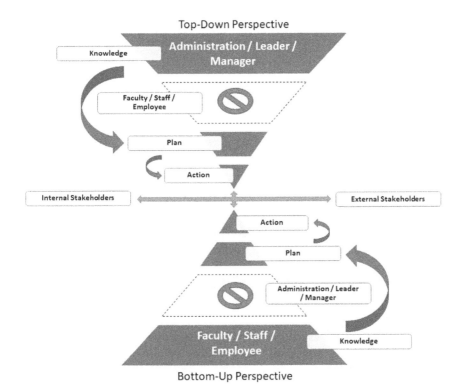

**Figure 10**  The devaluation of voice.

rulemaking when making a decision or form of negotiation to improve the value of voice. Next, informal agency rulemaking provides a government agency with gathering information in a more timely and efficient manner. Informal rulemaking by an agency involves gathering public comments through solicitation that is consistent with the Administrative Procedure Act (APA). The ability to determine the level and rules of the guidance allows the agency to informally decide how the rule should be made for the agency.

The first step in informal agency rulemaking is for the notice of the proposed rule to be published in the *Federal Register*. Second, a public hearing will take place. During the public hearing, all members will be allowed to witness the testimony of the pros and cons of the new proposed rule. Advocates will be subjected to cross-examination. When the testimony has been completed, an official transcript will be maintained. Third, the agency will publish the formal findings of the hearing based on the results. Finally, informal agency rulemaking will decide if the regulation should be disseminated and voiced to the public. The rule will only be published in the *Federal Register* if it is adopted.

Formal agency decision-making is made based on the records from proceedings and a trial. The first step in making a formal agency rule is for the agency to present the rule to the *Federal Register* publication so it can officially record the date and rule that was proposed by the agency. Next, formal agency rulemaking allows the interested parties to file any written comments related to the draft within a 30-day period from the posting in the *Federal Register.*

Based on the proposition, public hearing can also be held. Third, administrative agencies must post a response to the comments that were received and have raised a concern to the newly proposed rule. After addressing the comments, the final step an administrative agency must follow is to post a final draft in the *Federal Register* with a minimum 30-day period before the rule goes into effect. If changes are requested, collective bargaining or the negotiations process between the leader and members of the company will begin.

There are various approaches to creating value in the integrative negotiation process. The integrative negotiation process is utilized when two parties must rely on cooperation in order to achieve an agreement or a conflict resolution. When there is an integrative negotiation process, the negotiation is typically complicated and a long-term process with several issues to be addressed in the bargaining mix. In order to successfully implement the integrative negotiation process, the negotiator will need to establish the list of priorities for each individual. As a result, the negotiator must generate options within the negotiation process. The main goal of an integrative negotiation is to develop and create an alternative solution that provides additional value to both parties. This situation relies on the ability of the negotiator to be creative and to use their skills to develop potential new solutions.

Third, integrative negotiation relies on brainstorming. Brainstorming is an important tool for both parties to utilize when trying to classify each possible conclusion. New and unusual solutions are developed that will create undiscovered possible outcomes. The evaluation stage of the integrative negotiation process will be used to determine the success of each choice. As a result, the integrative negotiation process will enable individuals to develop long-term relationships for future agreements and contract decisions.

Finally, the integrative negotiation will establish a fixed-pie perception. A fixed-pie perception is the belief that when one person gains, the second party will lose. As a result, the fixed-pie perception in the integrative negotiation can create an obstacle to creating value. However, the negotiator can still claim value and enlarge the piece of the pie by avoiding reactive devaluation and defining a common goal and objective through the negotiation process. There are different methods of evaluating alternatives. The final step in integrative evaluations is claiming value and to evaluate all possible options. In order to help reduce the amount of negative emotions when entering into a new agreement, it is important to objectively evaluate the criteria of implementing each alternative or action.

The next method of evaluating alternatives is to avoid a win-lose situation. This situation causes the agreement of the negotiation to be undesirable to at least one party and to be accepted involuntarily. As a result, the level of competition between the two parties will result in a distributive bargaining process instead of an integrative bargaining process. Third, the outside standards of the situation should be considered when evaluating the alternatives. Outside standards are important when trying to develop a common level of standards. If there are no outside standards, then the negotiator will need to try and develop fair and equitable standards to achieving a high level of satisfaction for both parties. Fourth, reactive devaluation must be considered when evaluating alternatives. Reactive devaluation can occur when an individual makes concessions at the benefit of a second individual or party.

After the standards have been established, the negotiator will then evaluate the proposals of both parties. Evaluation of the proposals will analyze each issue in the bargaining mix and to develop a high level of interdependence between both parties. This strategy will help to establish a long-term relationship between both parties in order to promote future negotiations. Finally, each alternative needs to be clearly communicated and documented to both parties. This strategy will enable the negotiator to reach an agreed-upon understanding that will result in a written binding agreement. As a result, the negotiator will be able to overcome the dilemma of trust and honesty by establishing the guidelines and expectations of each alternative.

There are advantages and disadvantages of the various communication styles when it comes to negotiation. The first form of communication style is passive. Individuals who have a passive communication style typically have low self-esteem and a low self-worth. The advantage of passive communication is that it is used to avoid argument and confrontation. Individuals with a passive communication style will tend to agree with the group and to go along with the norms of the group. However, passive communication has the disadvantage of never breaking new ground in the negotiation process.

When the individual does not defend his or her beliefs, the group dynamic will never grow or change. Finally, passive communication can cause resentment and a further belief of low self-value based on the individual fear of sharing their opinions about an issue. The second form of communication style is aggressive. An aggressive communication style is used by individual to clearly express their feelings and need in a certain situation. Aggressive communicators will become strong advocates for a specific cause or belief. In order to support their belief, aggressive communicators will disrupt the rights of other individuals in order to gain what they believe is right. As a result, aggressive communication can be viewed as abusive to other individuals. The advantage of the aggressive communication style is that it promotes awareness of an issue or a situation. Individuals with an aggressive communication style will be useful in the negotiation process by defending their argument. The disadvantage of the aggressive communication style is that it creates a win-lose scenario. While one side will win the argument, it is usually at the expense of another individual. As a result, aggressive communication can lead to mistrust and sabotage by other individuals.

The final form of communication style is assertive. Next, assertive communication is guided by fairness, equality, and respect of other individuals and groups. The advantage of the assertive communication style is that it enables individuals to become connected with each other. Next, individuals are able to perceive a higher level of control within the situation and to address each problem as it is presented. However, the disadvantage of the assertive communication style is that it puts the locus of control on the individual. Failure to reach an agreement using assertive communication can cause the individual to become withdrawn and to incorrectly believe they deserve the outcome that was determined.

There are several barriers to communication that can impact the negotiation process. The first barrier to effective communication is the sender issues. The communication process begins when the sender encodes a message for the receiver. If the message in improperly encoded, the receiver will be unable to establish the actual beliefs and thoughts of the sender. This situation will cause the receiver to become ineffective in trying to "fill in the blanks" of the situation. The communication channel is determined by the habits and personal attributes of the sender. This situation can cause the sender to use the wrong communication channel based on their needs instead of choosing a method that would be more appropriate for the second party. As a result, the different level of interpersonal skills would cause a breakdown in the communication process.

The third barrier to effective communication involves receiver issues. When the receiver obtains the message from the sender, they can experience information overload. Information overload occurs when the amount of information is too large or great for the receiver to process. This situation will cause a delay in the negotiation process. Next, information overload will lead to ineffective communication based on the misunderstanding of the second receiver. The fourth barrier to effective communication is environmental issues. Environmental issues create noise and other mediums that distort the actual purpose of the message. Noise will lead to the distortion of the communication channel. Next, noise will cause both tangible and intangible barriers to the environment. The logistics, location and structure of the communication channel within an organization are important to understand so the negotiator is able to provide a clear pathway for open communication.

It is sometimes argued that a matrix organization can serve as a mechanism for achieving strategic fit—the achievement of process-synergies and communication methods across related business units resulting in a combined performance that is greater than the units could achieve if they operated independently. This situation enables a matrix operation to result in the achievement of strategic fit. A matrix organization is a combination of two different dimensions within an organizational structure that are used to complete a goal or objective.

A matrix organization will provide a firm to develop a flexible or an "elastic" business structure in order to change the configuration of resources to meet the changing demand of the market. Aligning the supply chain and competitive strategies will empower a firm to achieve an optimal level of production of outputs. The firm will be able to use a matrix structure to properly match the levels of staffing and resources to produce the desired number of outputs. The matrix structure within a firm will also help to reduce the amount of overhead and production costs of goods and services.

Next, a matrix organization will create a strategic fit through the achievement of synergies across related business units resulting in a combined performance that is greater than the units could achieve if they operated independently. When a firm is able to become flexible along two different dimensions, it will gain a competitive advantage. The firm will experience learned economies by having workers that are efficiently trained in different skills and can operate in various dimensions within the organizational structure. Each employee will be able to move through the matrix structure in order to complete the task at the optimum level of manufacturing high-quality outputs.

Finally, a matrix operation could result in the achievement of strategic fit by a firm's ability to become flexible and to adjust to the constant change in the economic environment. The more skilled workers become, the greater core competence a firm achieves. The firm is able to use learned economies to improve the economies of scale and scope. This strategy will enable a firm to maintain or increase its amount of market share. The firm will also be able to reduce the level of risk through the use of functional groups and projects. Staffing is constantly reevaluated and employees are reassigned to the necessary task. The firm will be able to reduce operational costs and operate at an efficient level. As a result, the matrix operation is able to continuously restructure the firm depending on the requirements of the project or economic environment.

It is important to understand the profiles of different generations at work, which create its own matrix operational structure within the company or the organization. In today's global economy, the workforce is formed by a combination of different age groups and generations. Each generation has its own unique standards and expectations. This situation will cause a company to employ individuals and employees who accurately reflect the diverse consumer base of the various market segments. With different generations in the workforce, there is a conflicting view of culture and how an organization should be structured.

There are four main generations in the workforce that include Veterans, Baby Boomers, Generation X and Millennials or Generation Y. Veterans began in the 1920s. The key characteristics of the Veteran generation is that they are hardworking, have strong attention to detail and do not like conflict. During the 1940s, the Baby Boomer generation began to enter the workforce. Baby boomers became more focused on service, providing feedback and being team players within the organization. In the 1960s, Generation X individuals entered the workforce. Generation X employees became highly adaptable to the changing market segments. Generation X employees were also independent and were extremely impatient when waiting for results. Finally, the Millennials entered the workforce after 1980. Millennials or Generation Y relied heavily on technology to improve the functions of the company. Next, Millennials had the ability to multitask and were financially aware of the expectations of the economy. Finally, Generation Y employees were optimistic about the future but required a great deal of supervision to remain on task.

It is important for managers and employees to understand the profiles of different generations at work in order to develop a diverse culture and to remain socially responsibility to each employee and consumer. Today, the veterans and baby boomers no longer have a high level of financial or corporate responsibility. The money and power of the organization and market have shifted to the newer generations of employees. This situation has the potential to cause conflict between the different needs of each generation. It is important for managers to understand the needs of each generation so the company is able to support each individual regardless of generation.

When a conflict does arise within an organization, the manager will need to understand the key characteristics and diverse needs of each generation. This strategy will enable the manager to accurately address the needs and concerns of each individual. Finally, managers within a company will need to be aware of how their actions and decisions are being perceived by the employees from each generation. The manager might have good intentions when making a decision that supports a generation of workers. However, the other generations might feel discriminated against and will become disloyal to the organization. It is extremely important for a manager to understand the history and needs of each generation in order to avoid potential conflict and issues in the organization.

Managers can use the ACORN principles to develop a strong sense of community and solidarity among all employee groups. ACORN is an acronym that is used to identify and describe the different principles managers can use to deal with the issues from the various generations in the workforce. The first stage is accommodating (A) employee differences. Accommodating employee differences enables managers to treat employees as customers in order to provide them the highest level of service with the company. The second stage is creating (C) workplace choices. Creating workplace choices will allow managers to determine what and how the work of employees can influence and change the level of satisfaction of the company.

The third stage is operating (O) from a sophisticated management style. A sophisticated management style will enable managers to be respectful and direct with every employee. The fourth stage is respecting (R) competence and initiative. Respecting competence and initiative will require managers to recognize and reward the best business practices and character traits from each generation in the workforce. The final stage is nourishing (N) retention. Nourishing retention involves the managers within a company to keep the best employees regardless of generational differences.

Managers must apply the method of the ACORN principles with effective communication throughout the company. This situation will enable managers to act fairly and to be socially responsible to each member of the company by making thought-out decisions and actions. Managers will be able to effectively communicate the overall expectations and goals of the company to each generation of employees within the company. Finally, managers will be able to use the ACORN principles to reduce the amount of conflict between employees in order to improve the efficiency and effectiveness of the organization.

Researchers at both the University of Michigan and the Ohio State University launched a major research effort directed at the identification of the behaviors associated with effective leadership. The research in predicting organizational effectiveness has changed from personality traits to the influence of behavior in order to impact the overall performance of the group members. The concept of leadership is only significant in the framework of two or more individuals.

Within a current organization, the behavior is based on usual task interdependence and frequent social interdependence. Usual task interdependence is based on the level of individual and group-member performance of pooled, sequential and reciprocal tasks within the organization structure. Frequent social interdependence is developed around the organizational structure that individuals are able to accomplish goals and objectives. The success of the leader–member process is dependent on the structure of the organization to complete tasks, along with the trust and behavior of the individual toward the final result or the outcome.

The results of the findings from the Michigan and Ohio State studies can both be compared and contrasted. The University of Michigan Research study analyzed the principles and various styles of leadership that led to a high level of employee job satisfaction and productivity. The study analyzed two main types of leadership styles.

Second, leaders can focus on production orientation which is a strategy that just focuses on the completion of tasks and ignores the needs of the employees within an organization. The Michigan research study also acknowledged that leadership is based on three main characteristics that include task-orientation, participation and relationship-oriented behaviors.

The Ohio State Leadership studies determined that there were nine dimensions of leadership that were divided into four categories. The leadership developed a 130-question questionnaire divided into 5 categories that produced 4 orthogonal factors; leadership is developed by an initiating structure that organizes behavior around a formalized structure within an organization where communication is based on job duties and level of authority. Third, leaders will focus on production emphasis, which is a behavior that uses the organizational mission to encourage and motivate the employees. The final factor is sensitivity. The leader's level of sensitivity is based on their ability to be socially aware of the needs of the internal and external environments.

The University of Michigan and the Ohio State University research studies are similar because both focus on determining the various characteristics of leadership. Next, both studies determined that all leaders fall into behavioral categories and exhibit a certain type of behavior based on the needs of the situation. However, University of Michigan and Ohio State University research studies also provided contrasting results. The University of Michigan research study concluded that leadership was a one-dimensional model. The success of the group would be based on the behaviors of the leader in the organization. The Ohio State University research study believed that leadership was multidimensional. Leadership was based on different behaviors and was directly linked to external variables. As a result, leadership is more complex, and different leadership styles will emerge to manage the particular situation and follow a path-goal approach.

The Path-Goal theory also determined that the behavior of a leader will be motivational and inspiring to the individual in order to improve efficiency and productivity within the environment. Leaders are required in the work-flow process to provide support and a motivational framework that assist in the group achieving the outcome or the goal. In order to improve efficiency, a leader must develop a behavior that influences the group to work toward a common path or a strategic vision.

There are four key leader behaviors identified in the Path-Goal theory of leadership. The first key behavior is leader directiveness. Leader directiveness will establish a positive link between the group members and the uncertain tasks and duties they are chosen to accomplish. However, leader directiveness can cause a negative relationship with group members if there is dissatisfaction within the assignment of clear tasks. The second key behavior is supportive leadership. A leader must show support in order to motivate employees to accomplish difficult duties and tasks. In order to increase motivation, the leader will need to establish milestones and provide rewards to celebrate and encourage success.

The third key behavior of leadership is achievement-oriented. Achievement-oriented leadership occurs when a leader establishes challenging goals and objectives for group members. To ensure the success of the group, the leader provides training and development of each individual in order to stress improvement and increased efficiency. An achievement-oriented leader will only accept the highest level of performance from each follower. The final key behavior of leadership is participative. Participative leadership is needed to understand the unique variables along with the individual traits in order to provide a participative framework. When the tasks are simple and repetitive, group members are the most satisfied since they focus on the task and not on individual ego or success. When the task is unusual and complex, group members also prefer this style because the leader will assist with the task in order for the specific individual to succeed and be recognized for their efforts.

The Path-Goal theory of leadership relates to the University of Michigan and the Ohio State University leadership studies. The studies determined that leadership resulted from the LMX process between the context of a situation and the characteristics and traits of the individuals involved. The Path-Goal theory of leadership combines the leader's concern for effectiveness with the behavioral concern for their employees. This strategy enables a leader to develop a framework between the task structure and the group members' satisfaction with their job.

Finally, leader directiveness will be most useful in a formal organizational framework with a tall hierarchy. Authority and structure are important variables to controlling and directing the workforce. Next, supportive leadership is based upon a leader setting a path or goal for an employee while providing the necessary training and resources to ensure the success of the individual.

Third, achievement-oriented leadership is most needed in a situation where the expectations of each individual are high and the maximum amount of effort is performed to achieve an ambitious goal. Finally, participative leadership is relied upon when the leader needs to have input from the group members in order to gather input and successfully achieve an objective or goal.

There are several major lessons about the follower that derive from the Path-Goal theory and LMX. The first lesson is that the action or inaction of a leader will have several effects on the social health or culture within an organization. Leadership is required to provide motivation and direction to the followers. A leader must understand the needs and perceptions of the followers in order to be effective and responsive to the various needs within the environment.

Next, the Leader Member Exchange (LMX) model is controlled by the contributions of the followers. Leadership cannot exist without a leader or follower. There must be a mutual exchange or benefit within a given situation. The perceptions and interactions of the followers will also define the leadership style and the qualities that are needed for goal achievement. A leader exhibits different qualities by stages in order to gain the support of the followers.

First, the followers will need to know that the individual chosen to be the leader wants the job. Next, the leader will need to influence the perception of the followers by communication and getting the job done. Third, the leader's actions must be consistent with doing the job in order to support the followers. Finally, the leader's action in the LMX model must demonstrate that they are able to maintain the job in order to remain responsive to the followers. The ability to maintain the job will involve transformational leadership by responding to the different traits and characteristics of the follower.

The LMX model also demonstrates the follower's impact on the organization by the need for mutual responsiveness. The relationship between the follower and the leader in the LMX model is reciprocal. In order to provide a successful leadership process, there must be synchronized actions and thoughts of the follower and leader. Next, the LMX model states that the relationship between a follower and leader is an active system. This situation enables the followers to be proactive and to influence the leadership process.

Finally, the perception of the leader's attributes will determine the follower's response to the decision or the action. The follower will use the LMX model to examine the leader's competence, motivation, and personality characteristics. The stronger the LMX process, the more idiosyncrasy credit the leader and follower will gain in order to create a more effective organization. As a result, the followers will influence the exchange process which will cause an individual to develop a transformational leadership style. This situation will allow the leader to provide a greater cultural understanding in order to meet the various needs of the follower and to form a mutual responsiveness in the social environment. The perceptions of the follower will be linked to the future success of a leader, based on their past results.

By drawing upon earlier readings as they pertain to LMX and leader effects, there are consequences stemming from the two faces of leadership. First, the positive face of leadership will rely on the LMX to enable the followers to institute levels of control over the leader. The LMX process "explores how leaders and managers develop relationships with team members; and it explains how those relationships can either contribute to growth or hold people back" (Mind Tools, 2015, para. 6). The positive face of leadership will enable the followers to influence the process based on the incorporation of their personal characteristics, traits and skills.

Next, leadership's positive face will use the LMX process in order to develop a synergy through the interactions of the leader and group of followers. A high level of synergy will enable the followers to perceive the actions of the leader as beneficial to the needs of the group. As a result, synergy will enable the leader to be successful based on the perceptions and willingness of the group members to follow the decision-making and actions of the leader. The positive face of leadership is influential in developing and stimulating a social good based on the needs and successes of the entire group. Finally, leadership's positive face will establish long-term relationships. This strategy will enable a leader to develop each group member and to utilize their unique skill set in order to become a more productive and effective team within the complex environment of the organization.

However, leadership's negative face will have adverse effect on the LMX process and the success of a leader. First, a leader will become controlling of the followers. Instead of being supportive of the needs of the group members, the leader will coerce each individual follower to follow his or her plan for personal gain regardless of the benefit to the group. Next, the dark side of leadership will cause a histrionic disposition. Leaders with a histrionic disposition will need to attract attention at all costs. This situation will cause a leader to overreact to the different variables in the environment. As a result, the decision-making process of the leader will become more self-serving instead of focusing on the needs and success of the group.

Third, the dark side of leadership will cause passive-aggressive behavior in the LMX process. Passive-aggressive behavior will develop in followers and will cause them to have negative and pessimistic behaviors about the actions of the leader. This situation will cause the leader to believe that the followers are supportive and complacent, but the followers will actually be secretly resistant to success of the leader. Fourth, the leader–member exchange process will be based on dependency. Finally, masochism will occur. Masochism occurs when the leader uses the LMX process to encourage a follower to take the blame for an action that was not their own. As a result, the follower receives the punishment instead of the leader as a result of poor decision-making or actions.

The two faces of leadership will be used in the LMX to classify the followers in the group. First, exemplary followers are encouraged by the leader to be independent, active and to use critical thinking as part of the decision-making process. Next, followers can be conformists. Conformists are dependent and active but do not possess the desire for critical decision-making. Third, followers can be passive. Passive followers are dependent on the leader, are reluctant to cause problems and have uncritical thinking ability. Fourth, alienated followers are passive, independent of the leader and possess critical-thinking abilities. Finally, followers can be pragmatists, meaning they possess a balance of activeness, dependence and critical-thinking abilities based on the needs of the particular situation.

There is a relationship among organizational theory, organizational design and change and organizational structure and culture. Organizational theory is important to understand the design and implementation of the business process to compete in today's market. It is the primary step in guiding the organization and determining the necessary changes to remain competitive. Organizational theory allows organizations to develop new ways to create equity for stakeholders and investors. Finally, organizational theory studies how business environment impacts the organization's business processes and how the function in its market segment.

Next, organizational design and change are needed to establish a successful organization. Organizational design is formal and the process that enables managers to monitor and control all aspects of the organization to achieve its objectives and goals. Organizational change is the method an organization uses to transfer from its current state of business operation to its desired level. Organizational change helps to increase the efficiency and effectiveness of the organization.

Organizational change and design is important at all levels within the organization. The management of organizational and design allows management to control all activities and functions of the business process. Next, organizational change and design balance the needs of the organization. Within every organization, it is important to understand the internal and external needs. Organizations that are able to control internal and external needs are able to increase its revenue, return on investment and are able to continue to compete in the future.

Third, organizational change and design are needed to enable the organization to continually redesign and reformat its business structure and strategy.

The ability to make changes to the business layout and strategy enables the organization to respond to the changes in the local and global markets. Adapting quickly to changes in the global business environment is important to being able to meet the needs of the changing demands of the consumer. Finally, managing the design and change of the organization enables the organization to reduce its amount of risk and helps to ensure a successful functioning business strategy and plan.

Organizational theory also includes organizational structure and culture. An organizational structure is how actions and resources are managed to achieve specific objectives and goals. Each level of the organization's structure is important from the chief executive officer to the front-line employees to coordinate actions and tasks. Any breakdown in the organizational structure will lead to a slowdown in production and will cause the company to lose revenue and market share. Finally, organizational theory studies the culture of the organization. The culture of an organization creates a social norm for the employees and allows consumers to know what they can expect from the company. The behavior of an organization determines how it will respond to the needs of the consumers and the surrounding business environment. The structure and culture of the organization are the means by which it is able to achieve its goals.

Organizational theory, organizational design and change and organizational structure and interrelated to each other. Together, each area works together to help form a cohesive business structure and strategic plan. Organizational theory and design create the social norm for a formal and informal organization. The business processes and use of resources are able to be properly managed. The organization's human resources and level of communication at every level are also improved with a strong structure, design and theory. Finally, business functions, organizational and consumer behavior, products and services and business markets can be managed to meet the changing needs of the consumer with organizational theory, organizational design and change and organizational structure.

There are several examples of how the interests of different stakeholder groups may conflict causing dissent and static so communication cannot be heard and voice to fall on deaf ears. The motivation of stakeholders is based on their return on investment or reward from the organization. Inducements to the stakeholder include status in the organization, position of power and monetary value. The contributions of the stakeholder include the knowledge and skills required to run and support the organization's goals and mission. Depending on the different types of stakeholders, the interest will vary depending on the specific group. There are two main types of stakeholders that include inside and outside groups. The inside stakeholders are the shareholders, managers and workforce. The outside stakeholders are customers, suppliers, government, unions, community and the public.

Shareholders are the actual owners of an organization. They have invested their money to make a profit in the particular organization. The main goal for the shareholder is to make money on their investment. While the shareholder provides the organization with money and capital, they expect to be compensated with quarterly dividends and increased stock value. The conflict that arises between shareholders and other stakeholder groups is that the shareholders want to make sure the company makes a profit. The shareholders want to guide the culture and influence the actions of upper management to meet their specific needs.

The interest of managers is to obtain salaries, bonuses, status and power within the organization. Managers provide the organization with their skills and knowledge of how to manage business processes and implement a strategic business plan. Managers conflict with other stakeholder groups in that they expect to earn both a monetary reward and "psychological satisfaction" from the organization. The interests of the workforce are to earn daily wages, bonuses, promotions and to have stable employment. The workforce provides the organization with skills and knowledge in a specific field helping to give the organization a competitive advantage. Employees who feel that they are not fairly compensated for their work will become dissatisfied, which will cause a conflict with the other stakeholders.

The first outside stakeholder group are the customers. Customers provide an organization with revenue and profits that come from the number of purchases of goods and services. To gain consumer loyalty and satisfaction, organizations must provide a high-quality good or service for a low cost. This strategy can cause a conflict with other stakeholder groups because it will decrease the profits, equity and return on investment. Suppliers guarantee that the organization will receive high-quality goods using quality control in the production of inputs. Suppliers demand a high level of revenue and return on investment for their ability to supply high-quality materials to the organization. This strategy could cause a conflict with other stakeholder groups in that the additional costs it takes to purchase high-quality raw goods will take away from the additional revenue desired by the managers, employees and other groups.

The third outside stakeholder group is the government. The government provides businesses and organizations with rules and regulations for good business practices. Government helps to ensure free and fair competition for every company. The government also has the power to punish organizations through fines and trade restrictions if laws are broken. The government and lawmakers can cause a conflict with the other stakeholders in that the rules they establish will limit the organization's ability to earn additional revenue and decrease its return on investment.

The fourth outside stakeholder group is trade unions. Trade unions provide organizations with fair and free collective bargaining power. The goal of trade unions is to guide and influence the productivity of the organization and the union. Trade unions expect to receive incentives for its union workers. This strategy will cause a conflict with other stakeholders because the negotiations, contracts and agreements with the trade unions will limit the organizations' ability to maximize its profits by controlling the business processes and strategy of the company to protect its own people.

The fifth outside stakeholder group is the community. Communities provide organizations with economic stability and a social structure. Local communities depend on organizations to increase the quality of living and level of employment in their area. Communities expect to benefit from the organization's revenue, employment and taxes it pays to do business. Organizations must satisfy the needs of the local community to succeed. Walmart (n. d.) stated that it "concentrates on helping people understand how families and communities can live better by using fewer natural resources, as well as growing healthy food in a more sustainable way" (para. 1). This strategy can cause a conflict with the other stakeholders because providing community support can be a time-consuming and expensive venture. However, failure to do so will lead to a decrease in profits and return on investment for all stakeholders.

The final outside stakeholder group is the public. The public provides organizations with customer loyalty and satisfaction. The public also helps to ensure that an organization has a strong and superior reputation over its competitors. The public supports both domestic products as well as the competition from foreign markets. The public expects organizations to enhance their national pride. Organizations in a certain market segment will provide the area with a positive or negative reputation. It is important for the organization to encourage support, donations and investment from the public to grow and compete in the global business market. This strategy can cause a conflict with the other stakeholder groups because it will require a lot of time, effort and financial resources to gain the acceptance of the public. Short-term profits will need to be reinvested into the organization decreasing the shareholder dividends and salaries for its workforce.

Bureaucracy is necessary in order for an organization to establish a structure so that the delegation of authority and tasks are appropriately assigned and distributed. There are six principles of bureaucratic structure, and there are several different ways that the principles of bureaucracy can help managers design the organizational hierarchy. The first principle of bureaucracy is based on the concept of rational-legal authority. Rational-legal authority is the amount of authority or control a person possesses with a predefined role or job title within the organization. Authority is given to a specific person based solely on the position he or she holds, not because of any personal attributes or characteristics. With rational-legal authority, all authority will be based on the position and not the individual who holds the particular station in the organization.

The second principle of bureaucracy is based on technical competence. Positions and roles within an organization are given only to employees who are capable of performing the job duties. Employees are not able to gain positions within an organization due to their social status, heredity or kinship. Assigning positions to employees who are competent of performing the task will eliminate risk to the organization and will ensure that business operations operate more efficiently and effectively.

The third principle of bureaucracy is that a role's task responsibility and decision-making authority and its relationship to other roles should be clearly specified. This principle is based on the concept of vertical and horizontal integration. Organizations will need to use vertical integration to determine the appropriate level and roles for decision-making within the company. Horizontal organization will help the organization to delegate the responsibility of tasks throughout the bureaucratic hierarchy. The role of task responsibility and decision-making authority needs to be clearly defined within the organization in order to eliminate role conflict and other potential internal environmental problems.

The fourth principle of bureaucracy is the organization of roles in a bureaucracy such that each lower office in the hierarchy is under the control and supervision of a higher office. Organizational hierarchy allows the organization to make employees accountable for their actions and to implement a greater level of control of its most valuable resources. It is important that each lower-level office directly reports to a higher office throughout the organization.

The fifth principle of bureaucracy is rules, standard operating procedures and norms should be used to control the behavior and the relationship between roles in the organization. Formal rules provide a written record of the expectations of the organization. Rules, standard operating procedures and norms also help to establish standardization among employees, managers and departments within the hierarchy of the organization. Finally, rules, standard operating procedures and norms help to integrate the different departments and coordinate the internal and external activities of the organization. The rules within an organization will help to control the culture and behavior of the overall organization.

The sixth principle of bureaucracy is administrative acts, decisions and rules should be formulated and put into writing. When the rules and regulations are put into a written document, they become an official document of the organization. Every action of the employee and organization are put into a written record that will help to train future employees. Written records are important because they cannot be overwritten and serve as a historical document for the organization. Together, these six principles help to improve the official structure and expectations of the organization.

To maintain structure and to establish a controlled form of communication, a level of bureaucracy needs to be established. Bureaucracy can become a problem within an organization. First, bureaucracy can cause a problem for managers and employees to follow the mission and vision of the organization. Rules should be established to help improve the business model instead of impeding the progress of the organization. The bureaucratic rules should help to enable the organization to achieve its stated goals and objectives. When rules prevent progress from being achieved, the top managers must reevaluate and define new rules in order to meet their goals.

Next, bureaucracy becomes a problem when the structure and regulations of the organization prevent managers and departments from expansion. With too much bureaucracy, the organization becomes inflexible. No changes can be made, and no growth will occur. The organization will develop a tall structure with many different levels of management to go through before completing a process. The decision-making will become centralized, leaving no room for improvement or new innovation. To prevent this situation from happening, the organization will want to make sure that it finds the right balance of rules and regulations that keep it focused on its goals while allowing the company to grow and expand into new markets.

Third, bureaucracy can eliminate new innovation in products or services. With too much bureaucracy, it will become too time-consuming and expensive to pursue a new idea. With the delay in the business process, the company will become slow to respond to the needs of the consumer and complex business environment. As a result of the slow decision-making and business process, the organization will lose market share and revenue. In order to prevent this situation from occurring, managers can work to implement new standard operating procedures and to streamline the business process so it is no longer delayed on arbitrary regulations in the organization's hierarchy.

Bureaucracy has the ability to rely too heavily on the rules of the organization. It does not give any thought to the process, growth or profit of the organization. As a result, the organization does not respond to the needs of the different stakeholders. In order to avoid this situation, managers must learn to monitor and control the hierarchy during the growth of the organization.

Establishing a bureaucracy that allows for growth will help to reduce the number of levels in the organization's structure. This situation will allow the organization to operate with the minimum number of levels needed to achieve its goals and objectives. Next, top managers can control the hierarchy by establishing a level of authority and control. Senior managers can be used to help make decisions and to decrease the amount of bureaucracy in the organization.

Organizations and companies will need to determine the right communication methods and processes that "fit" its culture and structure. Managers can establish a horizontal organization so employees can focus on completing tasks within the unit. This strategy will allow the organization to become more focused on producing outputs instead of being confined to only formal rules and regulations. Finally, managers can make the organization employee-oriented. Bureaucracy can cause employees to become distant or not feel that they are a valued asset. It is important to keep every employee involved in the organization in order to increase high-quality outputs and return on investment.

There is a relationship among creativity, intrapreneurship and innovation. Creativity enables organizations to create new ideas and product innovations that go beyond the current boundaries. Organizations operate in different paradigms such as technology, norms, beliefs, culture and knowledge. The introduction and implementation of a new idea or perspective will cause an organization to take advantage of creativity and to enter into new markets. Creativity is used to make or produce an output that is different than any of the previous products or services. Creativity can be simple or complex. It can also be inventive to provide a quantum technological change, or it can be innovative for an incremental technological change to an output. Finally, creativity is a personal process that comes from a specific individual. It cannot be compared to anything else that currently exists.

Intrapreneurship occurs when an organization encourages its employees to develop ideas for new products and services. While entrepreneurs create new inventions on their own, intrapreneurs are employed by top management to develop new innovations for their organization. Intrapreneurs use quantum and incremental changes to develop new or improve existing outputs. Intrapreneurship is responsible for the success or failure of an organization's product ideas.

Innovation is the process of converting an idea or invention into a good or service that creates value for an organization by providing a high-quality output for consumers to purchase. Innovation allows an organization to create and manufacture an output economically and efficiently. Innovation is important during the product life cycle. Every product will experience a change in demand over the course of its life. In the embryonic stage, innovation will develop a new product that consumers are not widely aware of. Next, a product will enter the growth stage where innovation will increase consumer demand. Third, a product will enter the mature stage where innovation of the product has peaked, and the majority of consumers have purchased the output. Finally, a product will enter the decline stage. During this stage, innovation is transferred from the existing product to a new product with quantum technology.

Creativity, intrapreneurship and innovation are similar ideas and concepts. Innovation and creativity expand the boundaries of an organization's knowledge. With creativity and innovation, organizations are able to use existing concepts in order to produce new ideas or outputs. As a result, modifications can be made to existing products while new product innovation can also occur. Intrapreneurship uses entrepreneurs who are employed within the organization to invent propriety goods or services. Intrapreneurship encourages an innovative culture and organic structure so new products and services can be created within the organization.

# Chapter 9

# CREATING THE NEW VOV LEADERSHIP MODEL IN ORGANIZATIONAL BEHAVIOR

The value of voice model of shared leadership does embrace the core tenets of shared leadership. Through an open process, stakeholders can at different times lead the work of the team and lead the shared discussions as a process to develop a broad set of facts that allow them to have greater understanding of the issues. The valuing of voice begins as an endeavor of vision. How the stakeholders and the leaders see what is important to the organization and its members must be determined. How can each stakeholder gain access to the vision?

The organization has specific cultural elements that each stakeholder works in to be productive and successful. The structural foundations of the organization will be central to how stakeholders will support the creating of the vision. It is the characteristics of the organization and the perceived essential conditions that shape experiences. The stakeholders live in the organization, and they have become part of the organization. What makes the organization special and valuable is the collection of experiences that the stakeholders will share with the team. The roles that each stakeholder has and their responsibilities in the organization are important to help further the continuous improvement of organization.

How the stakeholders interact and how they work to achieve their goals is through a shared process of inclusion. Including each stakeholder and valuing each member are what make the shared leadership and valuing of voice significant to the success of the organization. Inclusion of not just the stakeholder but also their lens and their share experiences must be incorporated into the overall voice of the organization and understood by all other stakeholders. It is because of these beliefs and the shared experiences stakeholders have already begun the work to value the individual voice. How stakeholders engage in this process is the cooperation that has been built by having a shared value of voice culture. A culture of cooperation is not just being polite; it is a system that respects each member, and because of this respect stakeholders can work as a collection of powerful change agents.

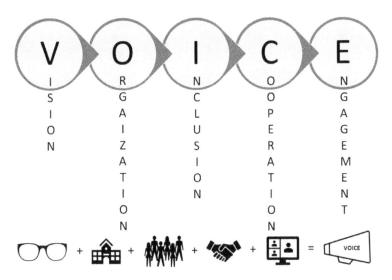

**Figure 11** The elements of voice.

The more the stakeholders can work to develop a system of cooperation and create a foundation for the organizational culture that honors and
respects each member, the better the collective solutions will be to address
issues and meet goal expectations. Organizations are not stagnant systems.
Organizations are constantly pushing and pulling stakeholders to move
toward change. External as well as internal forces are impacting organizations and drive change. If the stakeholders are operating in isolation, then
these moments of change will feel unattainable. Stakeholders will feel that
they cannot change or even possess the skills to change. If stakeholders are
working in a system that embraces cooperation and values and the individual
voice as part of the learning process, then the team will be able to weather
change. The idea of change will not seem to be so daunting because stakeholders will not feel alone in the process. They will realize that they are a
part of a larger team that is working collectively for the same outcomes.

As stakeholders are embracing cooperation and sharing voice, there is still
a need to focus on how each stakeholder is engaged in the work and engaged
with each other on the team. The organization as a system may place barriers
to engagement. School historically created barriers to engagement for staff.
Staff was grouped into specific roles and responsibilities, and there was limited sharing of information that may not be part of that group of stakeholders' roles. It is better for the organization to have ways to share information
and ways to embrace diversity so that all groups of stakeholders can work for
the collective good of the organization. As schools have evolved, the culture

within the schools has moved to embracing engagement of all stakeholders. For example, historically administrators hired key personnel for the school. This was done in isolation from other stakeholders and at the conclusion of the process the decision was announced.

Now for key staff acquisitions there are multiple different stakeholders who participate and share their evaluation of the candidate based on their lens and role within the organization. By engaging a variety of stakeholders with different experiences and expectations, a more reflective and representative decision process is used and hopefully a selection of the best candidate for the school.

The three criteria for determining whether a company has a winning strategy are the fit test, competitive advantage and performance. First, the fit test of the company needs to be divided into three parts to include external, internal and dynamic consistency. The company needs to make sure they are able to compete in the current and future market conditions. In today's economy, there has been a shift from large business to small business operations. The companies that have survived this paradigm shift have had to find ways to adjust to the external needs of the market and its consumers. Companies have to become more proactive and offer more attractive products to consumers in order to retain their business.

Next, companies need to make sure they have a strong internal fit within their organization. Companies need to make people their most valuable resources in order to run the business operations. This will ensure that the company's strategy is understood and executed accordingly. Third, a company needs to make sure that they are able to consistently compete dynamically in the business market. Given the changing nature of the economy, a company needs to have a winning strategy that will allow it to operate and to adjust to any potential market changes. If a company becomes static and does not change, they will be unable to compete with other companies and lose market share or go out of business.

The second criterion for determining whether a company has a winning strategy is competitive advantage. Competitive advantage is crucial to a company's winning strategy because it allows the company to have superior performance over other companies. When a company is able to perform a task to function better than their competitors, they have developed a competitive advantage. However, the company needs to ensure that they maintain their advantage. Once a strategy has been utilized, it can then be copied by other businesses and the competitive advantage will no longer exist. The key to maintaining a winning strategy is for the company to find a way to continuously develop and make their competitive advantage stronger and more productive so it outlasts the other businesses.

The third criterion for determining whether a company has a winning strategy is performance. The strategy of the company must produce strong performance levels in both competitive advantage and profitability. When a company is operating under a winning strategy, they are able to outperform their competitors. This situation gives the company ability to achieve a sustainable competitive in their business market and to establish a strong operational or product niche. The performance of a strong competitive advantage will allow the company to gain market strength and share. Second, the performance of a company's strategy will determine its level of financial profitability. The stronger the strategy of the company, the more of a competitive advantage they will have that will lead to a higher return on investment (ROI). High levels of customer retention, new customer development, increased market share and revenue are all signs of a winning strategy through ethics and the value of voice.

There is a difference between ethics and business ethics. Ethics focuses on the principles of right and wrong. The conduct of a person is based upon their own level ethics. What is right for one person may not be the same for another. Ethics are used to help an individual person decide what action is morally right and wrong. A person's ethics can vary based on their individual background, values and culture. They help individuals to establish goals and to determine the necessary actions needed in order to obtain the desired results. Ethics help to "police" individuals so they will not do anything they feel to be illegal or morally wrong.

Business ethics are similar to individual ethics in that they determine if an action is right or wrong. However, the main difference is that when a business makes a decision about its internal operations. Business ethics are the combination of the founders and core values of the organization. Each employee that works for the company is held to the same ethical standard the company has set for itself. The individual does not follow their own ethical code of conduct.

Business ethics deal with issues such as employee relations, sexual harassment and discrimination. How a business chooses to respond to these types of situations defines the ethical stance of the business. Next, business ethics help to set the boundaries of how a company does business with consumers, businesses and investors. Business ethics help to eliminate self-dealing managers that are focusing on their own interests instead of the entire organization. Second, business ethics remove the heavy pressure on managers to focus on short-term results. Managers are no longer just rewarded for achieving results, but how they achieved the results. Finally, business ethics establish a corporate culture that encompasses every employee. The performance of the business is put ahead of only achieving a high level of profitability with immoral actions.

Ethics and business ethics are similar in that they both deal with making right or wrong decisions. However, an employee's ethics might be different than the organization's code of ethics. When this situation happens, business ethics must be followed and the employee would have to make a decision based on the rules of the organization and not their own morals. Ideally, a person's ethics should mirror the business' code of ethics. Issues can arise when a company asks an employee to do something it believes is ethical, but the employee does not. This situation forces the employee to determine what action is right. If the organization does not have strong business ethics, an individual would have to lower their personal moral standards and do what the organization demands.

Business ethics are very important to a company. The higher the ethical standard a business can establish, the more respect there will be between the company and the consumer. Business ethics are needed to help a company become successful. In a global economy, there are many other competitors. Having a good ethical reputation is important to retaining and gaining new customers. Consumers must be assured that the business practices of a company are both legal and allow the company to be socially responsible.

Without business ethics, companies would experience three different costs. First, the visible costs for an unethical company would include government fines lawsuits. This situation would cause the stock price of the company to decrease and shareholders to receive smaller dividends. Second, there would be internal costs. Internal costs for unethical companies would include legal costs, corrective training and development and administrative costs to ensure ethical compliance. Finally, there would be intangible or less visible costs. These costs include the loss of consumers, loss of brand name recognition, recruiting costs, turnover costs and increased production costs. While ethics are important on an individual level, business ethics are needed to govern all processes and decisions of an entire company so that it can operate as one cohesive unit. Business ethics help to create the solution for any dilemma a company might experience.

Ethical standards impact the tasks for crafting and executing strategy. When a company is crafting and executing a strategy, ethical standards must be taken into consideration. Before crafting and executing strategy, the leaders of the company must make sure that the proposed course of action fully adheres to the company's code of ethics. Any action that is taken for crafting and executing strategy must meet the established code of ethics. If the new action does not, then the company is not operating under the original moral guidelines. Next, ethical standards will impact strategy by making sure that there is anything that could be considered ethically objectionable. If there is any part of the new action that would cause the strategy to not be ethical, then the action should not be carried out. Only ethical practices based on the business ethics established by the company should be implemented.

The next impact that ethical standards have on impacting the task of crafting and executing strategy is to make sure that the new action is in sync with the company's core values. The core values of a company are very important and set the expectation for every employee to follow. If the proposed action deviates from the existing core values, employees will begin to become self-dealing and the greater need of the company will be ignored. The fourth impact of ethical standards and their impact on crafting and executing strategy are to ensure that there are no apparent concerns or conflicts that could arise from the decision.

In order to make sure that the company's code of ethics is currently being met, the new crafted and executed strategy would have to undergo a litmus test. The litmus test is important in evaluating the three stages of any business strategy: first, the litmus test needs to verify that the proposed action is in compliance with the current code of ethics. If it is not, then the action should not be continued. If the action is in compliance with the code of ethics, the company must then determine if there is any ambiguity or uncertainty to the new action. If there is any uncertainty, then the necessary rules and regulations must be established so the wrong behavior is not rewarded. This strategy will help to ensure that the focus is on overall quality and reliability instead of short-term profitability.

The second stage of the litmus test is to verify that the proposed action is in "harmony" with the existing core values. Any action on behalf of the company should be focused around carrying out the mission of the company. The core values are important to determining every action of the company. If the action is not in harmony with the core values, the proposed action should not be carried out. If the action is in harmony, then the company needs to make sure that there are no potential conflicts or problems for its business operation. Potential conflicts and problems would need to be addressed. This strategy would ensure that every employee is on the same page and in harmony with the overall needs of the company.

The third stage of the litmus test is to determine if the desired action for crafting and executing strategy is ethically objectionable. If the investors and stakeholders find the proposed action objectionable, it should be discontinued. The proposed action must also be found socially acceptable by the social media and local communities. If the action is not widely accepted, it should not be carried out. However, if the proposed action is not considered objectionable, then the action should be implemented and carried out as a new strategy for the business.

The litmus test is a very important tool in determining how ethical standards impact the tasks of crafting and executing strategy. Ethical standards are necessary at evaluating the decision and use of all actions that are used to execute a business strategy. Ethical standards are necessary in making sure that the proposed action is honest. Second, the proposed action must be legal and conform to the stated government legislature. Third, ethical standards are needed to ensure that the decision can be executed with a good conscious. If there are uncomfortable feelings within the company by completing the action, then it would need reconsidered. Fourth, the proposed action would need to be proven ethically acceptable in the public eye. A company would need to be able to justify its action and demonstrate that it has nothing to hide by its chosen strategy. Finally, ethical standards impact the crafting and executing of strategy by determining the consequences of company's actions. The mental and physical impact of the new strategic action will need to be considered. If the action passes all of these factors, then the company was successful in crafting and executing a strategy with strong ethical standards.

The business environment and the tasks of management are expected to change over the next 30 or more years. The main change will be due to the change in the demographic of the environment. As a result, the baby boomer generation is pushing down the overall participation. This situation currently lowers the unemployment rate since jobs are being held for a longer period of time. However, when the baby boomers retire, the unemployment rate will increase and the younger generations will become the dominant demographic in the workforce. Next, since the baby boomer generation remained in their current positions for an extended period of time, the younger workforce will be inexperienced and unable to handle the workload. Next, the workforce will continue to change with the continued growth of women and minorities in the workforce. As a result, the workforce will become more diverse and global competition will increase.

Third, the business environment and the tasks of management are expected to change over the next 30 or more years due to new technology. Computers, telecommunications and information technology infrastructure has made it possible for small businesses to compete globally. The cost of modern technology has also significantly decreased allowing small businesses to equally compete with larger firms. Both large and small businesses will experience improved communication and expansion into new markets. However, the reliance solely on technology could lead to isolation or fragmentation between the firm and the consumer due to a lack of in-person customer service or support.

Finally, the business environment and the tasks of management are expected to change over the next 30 or more due to the evolution from the product to the service sector of the market. The service industry is growing more rapidly and is responsible for the majority of revenue in the economy. With the more service-based companies, unions will increase to protect the rights of the employees. This situation could lead to more political turmoil and government intervention. Finally, the income level for various positions will decrease. As the quality of life increases, employees will become more skilled. The workforce will become saturated with trained professionals. This situation will result in firms being able to hire the most skilled candidate for the lowest price causing a disparity income from the previous workforce generation.

When a company is named to one of the "best giving voice in socially ethical responsibility" lists, it can potentially reap several positive effects. First, a company that is named to one of the "best giving voice in socially ethical responsibility" lists will experience an increase in trust and loyalty from consumers and investors. The company is able to become more efficient and to increase its market share through consumer satisfaction. The image and brand name recognition increases due to the high level of quality and standards. The firm will reap the benefit from long-term business relationships with suppliers, distributors, consumers and stakeholders.

The second positive effect a company can reap when it is on the "best in social responsibility" list is investor loyalty. Investor loyalty will improve by a company gaining the advantage of maintain its original investors while establishing new relationships with potential investors. The more socially responsible an organization becomes, the more value it will offer the consumers in the market segment. This situation will result from the implementation of a strong corporate culture that is built on high operational standards of quality and the ability to rely on ethical decision-making. As a result, the company will experience an increase in profits and shareholder wealth creating the desire for continued and improved investor loyalty.

The third positive effect is commitment. A "best giving voice in socially ethical responsibility" company will experience an increase in support from employees. When a firm becomes socially responsible, the employees will become more valued and dedicated to the success and quality of the company. Employee morale will increase causing an escalation in productivity and standards of quality. Fourth, a "best in social responsibility" company will experience an improvement in Consumer Relationship Management (CSR). Consumers of a socially responsible company will have a life-long or long-term loyalty based on the high level of commitment and quality of the goods or services. Consumers will trust the actions of the company to provide goods and services that will improve the quality of life at a fair or reasonable price.

Fifth, a company may earn a tax benefit from the local, state and federal government. When a company shares its value of voice and implements business processes that protect the consumers and the environment, it will receive special inventive and tax breaks for being socially responsible. Finally, a "best in social responsibility" company will lead to an increase in profits and revenue. The more socially responsible an organization becomes, it will experience improved efficiency that will lead to economies of scale, scope and learned economies. As a result, the company will become highly efficiency and able to reduce the cost of production, reduce risk and to increase profits.

However, there are also possible costs or negative outcomes that may be associated with being named to one of these lists. First, social responsibility requires a hard commitment and investment by a company. The company on a "best giving voice in socially ethical responsibility" list will need to devote the necessary time, resources, and money to continue to support the environment. Next, a high level of social responsibility will cause a company to experience an increase in costs. Since the economy is expanding globally, the responsibility of a company will continue to increase. As a result, the cost of production of outputs will increase causing a decrease in profits.

The third possible cost or negative outcomes that may be associated with being named to one of these lists is a conflict of achieving corporate goals while remaining socially responsible. Companies are created to sell goods and services that will provide revenue for the shareholders. When a company invests in highly socially responsible programs, the amount of profit is reduced to fund the initiative. Stakeholders who are profit seeking may not support the large cost associated with social responsibility. Although the shareholders support the benefits of social responsibility, they might not approve of this level of commitment. Finally, shareholders and investors will believe that the company is overspending or mismanaging funds to support social responsibility initiatives that cause a decrease in profits and stock dividends. As a result, the company will become less effective and efficient due to the conflict between the goals of the shareholders and the top management team of a "best in social responsibility" company.

Various business disciplines, including marketing, finance, accounting and human resources, have an important role in social responsibility. Different disciplines bring specific views and philosophies to the implementation of social responsibility. The various business disciplines need to work together to provide a course of action that enables a business to generate revenue and profit for shareholders. A business has a social responsibility to all of its various shareholders that include consumers, investors, employees, suppliers, distributors and the local community. The actions of the company stakeholders must be ethical and socially responsible to the consumers and community it supports.

The socially responsible actions of the company are carried out through the marketing, finance, accounting and human resources divisions. Marketing plays an important role in social responsibility because it communicates the quality of the output to the consumer. Marketing will enable the business to effectively promote and price goods and services at a reasonable price for consumers. The firm will use marketing to be socially responsible by communicating the safety warnings, concerns and specifications of the output. Marketing will also be used to communicate and follow up with the consumer after the initial purchase of the output.

Next, finance is important to the social responsibility of a company. A business must use financing to ensure that the necessary funds are available to invest in innovations and product development. Financing is also required for a business so it can determine the amount of funds required to provide the desired level of social responsibility to the community. Socially responsible companies also use finance to gain the trust and support of investors for future business practices. The more socially responsible a company becomes, the more investors will be willing to make long-term investments. This situation will help to provide a company with a strategic advantage over competitors and to ensure its success in the future with ethical decision-making.

Third, accounting is important discipline for socially responsible companies. Accounting is necessary for a business to ensure that the financial information is recorded accurately based on the Securities and Exchange Commission. Socially responsible companies need to ethically and accurately report the revenue and losses to provide investors with the correct information. The financial situation and conditions of the company must represent the "true" state of the company to remain socially responsible to the rate of return for investors. Fourth, human resource is required for an organization to be socially responsible. The human resources division of a company will help to provide a safe and secure work environment for the employees. Human resources will also enable the company to develop policies and procedures that are fairly applied to each employee. As a result, the company will make ethical business decisions and have a culture of respect and equality. Employees will experience an increase in trust and will become more invested in the company due to the role of social responsibility.

There are two types of effects of leader behavior and the value of voice through the actions of the leadership. The first leader behavior is a direct effect. Based on the behavior of the leader, the follower will learn the culture of the organization. The direct behavior of the leader will also influence the actions and thought process of the follower. Leaders with a direct effect of behavior will be more controlling in nature. The organization will have a tall structured hierarchy in order to implement formal levels of control. The leader's behavior will be determined by a current action instead of the possibility of what will happen. As a result, the leader will have a direct impact on the success and satisfaction of the individual.

Indirect leader behavior is concerned with the possible "implications" or potential outcome of a situation. The leader will develop behavior based on his or her perception of the event that will occur, instead of what has previously transpired. As a result, indirect leader behavior will be used to help guide and influence the "in-group" of followers to achieve a goal. Indirect leader behavior develops within an organization that has little authority and uses substitutes for leadership as an alternative to a direct formal leader.

There are several differences between direct and indirect effects of leader behavior. First, the behavior of a leader is reciprocal and can also be dependent based on the performance and satisfaction of the follower. Direct leader behavior will dictate the satisfaction and actions of an individual. However, indirect leader behavior will be developed based on the employee's past performance and the leader's perceived ability in the follower to complete a future task. As a result, both direct and indirect leader behaviors provide a causal effect to the level of employee satisfaction and the effectiveness of an organization. Direct leader behavior will guide the employee's current actions, while indirect leader behavior will influence a future decision.

Next, there will be a direction of causality between the leader and the follower with the use of substitutes of leadership. The quantity and interaction of various complex variables of an event will be determined by the need for direct or indirect leader behavior. In a situation where the goal is easily obtainable, the leader will be able to use substitutes of leadership and direct leader behavior. However, if the leader is unsure of the success of the goal, he or she will use an indirect effect in order to ensure the success of the event by using other methods to achieve the achievement of the goal. There will always be a cause-and-effect relationship between the leader and the follower based on the strength of the team or substitute resources to complete the task and avoid neutralizing factors.

Finally, the leader will need to determine the need for direct and indirect leadership based on the number of substitutes required for each individual in order to motivate and increase productivity while decreasing the neutralizing factors in the environment. While both direct and indirect leader behavior influence the satisfaction and efficiency of the follower, effective leadership will only occur when the right behavior is used in a given situation. As a result, direct and indirect leader behavior is required to create an organizational culture with an established leadership style and to form a direct link to providing employee satisfaction and increasing the overall effectiveness of the organization.

There is a relationship between the substitutes for leadership and employee job attitudes, role perceptions and performance. There are many different variables that can be used as a substitute for leadership. This situation will cause the emergence of either a direct or an indirect leader behavior, based on the complexity of the environment. The performance and satisfaction of the follower will be established by their perceptions of the behavior of the leader. As a result, there will be potential for a high level of ambiguity in terms of supportive leader behavior.

Role ambiguity can occur due to a follower's lack of clarity of under-standing about the expectations of duties, behavior and status within the organization as a result of the leadership's lack of voice. When there is a poor understanding of the expectations within an organization, the follower will be unable to develop the proper traits and characteristics in order to succeed. There will be confusion regarding the role of the employee. The employee will not be able to conform or adjust to the culture of the organization. Due to the high level of ambiguity, the follower will be unable to properly understand or support the vision of the leader.

In order to reduce the level of ambiguity, in terms of supportive leader behavior, organizations will need to implement formalized written policies and procedures; doing so will create a strong organizational structure and will clearly define the rules and responsibilities of each person. Next, leaders can use substitutes to leadership such as creating cohesive teams within the organization. Organizations with a team environment will have less ambigu-ity, and each follower will be involved in the successful achievement of the goal. Third, leaders must provide feedback to each supporter. Feedback is important because it allows the follower to understand their level of role per-formance and satisfaction within the organization.

Leaders will need to clarify the expectations of the follower within the organization. The more clarification a leader can provide, the less ambiguity will occur in the work environment. When there is a low level of ambiguity, the supporter's attitude toward their role will improve. The supporter's atti-tude and behaviors will also become more positive and focused on achieving the goal of the organization, instead of only focusing on their individual suc-cess. A high level of ambiguity will also lead to role conflict and in-role perfor-mance issues. Leaders need to establish a valid reward system that supports the right behavior required to manage the different variables.

Altruism can be used to eliminate ambiguity by becoming a substitute for leadership. Altruism will help to focus each supporter to act for the well-being of the entire group instead of only themselves. Ambiguity can also be eliminated in order to support leadership by conscientiousness. Conscientiousness occurs when a supporter is aware of the different needs of the leaders and other supporters in the organization and only performs actions that benefit the group. Sportsmanship is also required in order to support leadership. Since organizations operate in an imperfect environment, leaders and supporters must work together to overcome any uncertainty and challenges that will arise. Finally, courtesy and civic virtue are necessary to form strong relationships so the leader and supporters can spend more time working on meaningful tasks that will benefit the entire organization.

Charismatic leadership is when a leader is able to use their personal characteristics and traits in order to influence or "charm" a group of followers to gain their support during a situation or an event. A charismatic leader relies on their personality and uses their strong self-image instead of formal authority to guide individuals to complete a goal or a task. Charismatic leadership relies on the LMX process based on the traits of the leader and the behavior and willingness of the followers to support his or her actions. Transformational leadership and charismatic leadership are required to help bring a change within an organization by gaining the support of the followers during a complex and difficult environment.

There are several characteristics of a charismatic leader and the components of the charismatic leadership process. First, charismatic leadership is based on the past history and knowledge, skills and abilities that are perceived by the group of followers. However, in order for a leader to demonstrate charisma, there must be relationship between the traits of the leader and the particular situation in order to gain the support of the followers and form a strong "in-group." A strong component of charismatic leadership is the ability of an individual to focus their knowledge and actions to conform to the needs of the current situation.

Next, the charismatic leadership process requires a strong relationship between a leader and at least one follower. Charismatic leadership cannot exist without a follower or a situation that requires the need for a leader. As a result, there is a dynamic relationship between the leader, follower and the situation. While the follower may not originally agree or understand the goal or the objective, they will be drawn to the aura of the leader and will blindly follow them based on the force and influence of their personality and beliefs. Charismatic leaders are intense about their actions. The intensity of a leader causes them to be extremely loyal and passionate about their cause. This situation will cause followers to become emotionally involved and invested in the desired goal achievement of the leader.

The main characteristic of a charismatic leader and the components of the charismatic leadership process is a high level of self-confidence. Charismatic leaders possess the ability to trust in knowledge and skills in order to overcome the challenges of any complex situation. Second, the charismatic leadership process requires the leader to have a strong conviction and belief that their actions are right. The ideas of the leader are believed to be correct and the best course of action by the followers. Finally, charismatic leadership relies on dominance. Dominance is the strong influence and power an individual has in order to overcome objection and doubt of the followers in order to gain their support toward achieving the desired goal or objective in a complex environment.

Transformational leadership is a leadership style that inspires trust between the leader and group of followers in order to achieve a desired goal. Transformational leadership will enable a leader to use their knowledge, skills and abilities to influence the followers and to develop a supportive "in-group." A transformational leader will be able to motivate and inspire other employees to focus on their strategic goals and vision for the benefit of the entire organization.

Transformational leadership will provide an increased level of consideration by the leader and improved satisfaction from the followers by giving and lending their value of voice. When there is a higher level of trust, respect and consideration from the leader, the followers will gain more confidence. As a result, the performance level of each follower will increase, making the organization more effective. Based on the situation, a leader is able to use transformational leadership to manage the variables for goal achievement. The leader will also use a cross-cultural perspective to better understand the group of followers, so there is a higher level of perceived leadership.

There are many different dimensions of transformational leadership. First, transformational leadership enables each individual within the group to determine the collective capability to perform the tasks and duties in order to achieve the desired outcome. This situation enables the individual followers to analyze and think about the critical needs of the group and to determine innovative solutions to the complex problems in the environment. As a result, the higher level of collective efficacy within the group, the more cohesive and productive the organization will become in the achievement of the outcome. Next, transformational leadership creates respect between the leader and the follower. Over time, the leader and the follower are able to gain loyalty and trust based on the performance results and success of achieving the objective or goal.

Another dimension of transformational leadership is that leaders using this method will be able to influence the perceptions of withdrawal behaviors from group members. In order to eliminate withdrawal behaviors, the leader must inspire confidence and respect to each group member in order to increase the level of loyalty and trust with the individual. Trust is also necessary to establish transactional and transformational leadership. Transactional leadership focuses on formal authority and defined roles of individuals within an organizational setting.

This form of leadership will enable the leader to manage employees based on a series of fair rewards and discipline based on individual actions. Transformational leadership requires a leader to gain trust from their followers to identify the need for change and to inspire a new vision to implement the necessary change. The final dimension of transformational leadership enables the leader to guide and persuade the "in-group" of followers to express their ethics and beliefs by directly connecting them to the vision of the organization. A strategy will need to be created and exist to establish mechanisms within the organization that all the individual to directly identify with the vision through values, beliefs, culture and share group interests.

Transformational leader behaviors are used as part of the exchange process between a leader and a group of followers in transactional leadership. The leader's transformational behavior will establish the reward system that will be used to encourage the followers to improve their level of performance to achieve the goal or objective. These transformational behaviors of the leader establish a higher order of needs for the group and cause each member to self-sacrifice in order for the greater good of the entire group.

Transformational leader behaviors also influence individuals to take on extra roles within the organization to benefit the society of the group. First, a leader can use direct transformational behaviors in order to use formal authority and organizational structure to influence the desired level of performance conscientiousness of each individual with the society or hierarchy. Next, a leader can use indirect transformational behaviors. Indirect transformational behaviors are used to develop trust and loyalty from followers within an organization based solely on the level of perception and supportiveness of the leader.

There are six transformational leader behaviors that can be measured that include identifying and articulating a vision, providing an appropriate model, fostering the acceptance of group goals, high performance expectations, providing individualized support and intellectual stimulation. First, identifying and articulating a vision is an important behavior of a transformational leader. Identifying and articulating a vision is important to recognizing new and innovative opportunities for the leader's group of followers. However, a leader must also be able to share his or her vision with the other individuals within the organizational structure in order to continue to motivate and inspire future success and goal achievement.

The second transformational leader behavior is providing an appropriate model. Providing an appropriate model enables the leader to establish a formal structure for the individuals to follow. This strategy is important because it provides a framework that is designed to ensure the success of the group members so the organizational goal or vision of the leader can be accomplished. Providing an appropriate model also allows the leader to combine the values of the entire group with the vision in order to provide a higher level of group satisfaction and productivity. The third transformational leader behavior is fostering the acceptance of group goals. This behavior is important because it will enable the leader to encourage and promote teamwork and a high level of cooperation between the group members. As a result, the lead and "in-group" of followers will be able to work more cohesively to achieve the current goal. Transformational behaviors will show the leader's consideration for the needs of the group, allow the group to become innovative, to share in the organization's vision and act as role models to improve productivity and performance.

Transactional and transformational leadership can be compared and contrasted. Transactional leadership is used by leaders who motivate employees with rewards and punishments. This form of leadership works best in organizations with a tall structure and hierarchy. Organizations that are autocratic in nature will acknowledge the contributions of employees based solely on their results and level of productivity. When an employee is able to demonstrate a high level of performance, he or she will become part of the leader's "in-group." However, if an employee is perceived to have a poor level of performance, the leader will not recognize their contributions, and the individual will be punished and become part of the "out-group."

Once again, this new strategic model of leadership combines six transformational leader behaviors that include identifying and articulating a vision, providing an appropriate model, fostering the acceptance of group goals, high performance expectations, providing individualized support, and intellectual stimulation. Next, transformational leadership is a leadership style where the leader is responsible for recognizing the need for innovation and change. The leader is also tasked with creating a vision to guide the change through motivation, inspiration and executing the change with the help and support with the group of followers.

Transformational leadership focuses on task performance. When a follower demonstrates positive characteristics and skills, he or she will be recognized for their efforts by the leader. However, transformational leadership focuses on Organizational Citizenship Behavior (OCB). OCB works to enhance job performance and satisfaction by creating a positive psychological and social culture in the organizational environment. Transformational leadership enables a leader to inspire the followers to combine their internal interests to match those of the entire group. This strategy creates a team environment that improves the LMX process.

Finally, transactional leadership is not focused on the future goals of the organization. Instead, transactional leaders are concerned with the success of the current business operation. The main concern of transactional leaders is to provide maximum efficiency for the organization in the current environment and to maintain the normal business operations. Transformational leadership focuses on the current success of the organization while also developing new innovative ways to ensure the success of the group in future situations. In order to achieve future success, transformational leadership sets goals, incentives and establishes a reward program to encourage the followers to perform at higher a higher level. This situation allows the leader to provide each individual within the group with the opportunity for future personal and professional growth within the organization.

There are individual and organizational effects that are seen as being associated with the presence of the transformational leader. First, individuals will experience the effect of improved task performance through the LMX process. Second, the presence of a transformational leader will improve the OCB. This situation will eliminate the belief of obligations or the need to provide gifts or favors in order to gain individual success. Instead, individuals will be encouraged to denounce their own self-interests and to focus on the success of the entire group.

The third effect of transformational leaders is that there is an enhanced or improved level of receptiveness among the followers of the group. When there is a level of loyalty and trust between the leader and group members, each individual will be more open and accepting to follow the leader, based on the results of past experiences. As a result, each individual is able to gain new behaviors that will enable him or her to play an important role and to define the culture of the group based on their social identity within the organization.

The fourth individual and organizational effects that are seen as being associated with is the presence of the transformational leader that the LMX process becomes more personal to both the group and the individual. When a leader is able to use transformational leadership to motivate each individual, the follower will become more directly invested in the goals of the organization. As a result, the entire group will share the same core values and goals. Under the transformation of the leader, the group will become more productive and will focus on achieving the same vision or goal.

Transformational leadership will positively impact task performance and the individual's OCB. This form of leadership will also directly influence the LMX between task performance and individual satisfaction within the organization. When each follower is able to feel more valuable, he or she will become more invested in the goals of the leader and will improve their level of efficiency. This situation will lead to the successful achievement of the objective or goal.

Transformational leadership behaviors will act as social currency in order to increase the LMX process. The more social currency that is earned, the more receptive each individual will become to the expectations of the leader. Finally, the LMX process provides an organizational framework and culture that make transformational leadership more directly important to each follower in the group. This strategy will work to develop the leader and group of followers in order to increase productivity and to successfully achieve the goal of the organization.

There are also several ways an organizational culture can increase organizational effectiveness. First, culture increases organizational effectiveness with the use of motivation. With clearly defined norms, beliefs and values organizations are able to provide employees with the tools required to succeed. Employees who embrace the culture of the organization will gain more property rights within the organization. Organizational culture will also motivate employees by offering intrinsic and extrinsic rewards and incentives. The more motivated and invested the employee, the more the organization will experience an increase in core competencies and will also gain a competitive advantage of its competitors.

Second, culture will improve the organizational structure within a company. It is important for the culture and structure of the organization to complement and support each other. The structure of an organization will work to establish the terminal values that need to be achieved. The desired level of excellence, innovation, profitability, quality and reliability will be increased by the use and implementation of culture. Third, organizational culture will increase effectiveness by using instrumental values to guide the behavior of every employee.

The instrumental values are important to organizational effectiveness because they stress the belief in hard work, dedication and the acceptance of norms and traditions of top management. Together, terminal and instrumental values will work together to emphasize the norms of the organization. The structure of the organization will also be influenced by the culture. Organizations can either utilize a tall or flat structure. Tall organizations will be mechanistic. With a mechanistic structure, decision-making is centralized. The objectives and goals of the organization are standardized.

As a result, the outcome and end results are predictable to all employees and managers within the organization. Organizations that institute an organic structure will have a flat hierarchy. Decision-making will become decentralized and widespread throughout the organization. The culture of the organization will need to mirror the needs of the structure. For an organic organization, the culture will need to promote innovation and creativity. Employees will need to be in an environment that supports flexibility in finding new business processes and contingency plans.

It is very important to obtain the right fit between organizational structure and culture. Organizational structure will affect the culture within the company. The way that the tasks and workflow is completed will be determined by the level of acceptable behavior. The culture must set the guidelines to support the structure within the organization. If the culture fails to support the structure, the organization will experience disharmony and unethical practices that do not match the beliefs of the founder or the top management. Organizational structure and culture must also find the right fit in order to create a successful business strategy and strategic vision. The core competencies continue to grow and expand giving the organization an increased market share over its competition. The culture will also support the structure of the organization by utilizing its employees as a resource and core competency.

Organizations that are able to find the right fit will be able to have fully invested employees which will strengthen the norms and the values. Finally, the right fit between culture and structure will improve the flow of communication, the reporting relationship and the completion of tasks within the organization. When the communication is improved, all levels within the organizational hierarchy will be able to work more efficiently. Goals, tasks, duties and expectations will be clearly defined and stated for each position. As a result, the organization will be able to increase its level of efficiency and will produce higher-quality outputs.

Organizational structure is a succession of various methods and techniques that managers use in order to increase the success of the organization. With the use of various methods and techniques, organizations will become more flexible and able to adapt to meet the changing needs of the environment. Top management achieves organizational change and development with the use of the action research method to minimize the gap between the actual and desired state of the company.

One of the goals of organizational development is to eliminate the resistance to change. Resistance for change can cause problems throughout the entire company structure and hierarchy. Organizational development will work to improve communication between the internal and external environments of an organization. Participation and empowerment of employees will also increase. Employees will become more invested and increase their level of involvement as the organization develops to its desired state. Facilitation will occur between top management and employees to promote flexible team-building in order to produce an efficient business process.

Next, organizational development is necessary to help employees within an organization to reach their desired potential through the value of voice. New goals and objectives are determined for the organization that will help it expand and grow within the business market segment. Organizational development will foster new activities such as training, performance rewards, team-building exercises and an improved level of communication. Process improvements will also improve due to organizational development. As the organization grows, the culture of the organization will change to focus on the consumer instead of the product. The new business process will focus on producing the products consumers want instead of what the business currently manufactures.

The goal of organizational development is to improve the efficiency and effectiveness of organizations. It also will help top management to identify and assign duties and tasks to specific individuals in the output process. As a result, organizations will become more streamlined and efficient. Organizations will overcome their resistance to change and increase their potential of producing high-quality outputs, resulting in greater core competencies and competitive advantage. As a result, each organization will be able to produce a higher quantity of outputs and to increase its ROI to its stakeholders.

The design of the organization's structure and culture are able to give subunits more power with the control in several different ways. First, the organization's structure and culture will enable subunits to have more control over valuable resources and raw materials. With the control of valuable resources and raw materials, subunits are able to improve their performance and to increase their level of indispensability. The more indispensable a subunit becomes to an organization, the more resources it will obtain, and it will also become a core competency to the organization.

Second, the organization's structure and culture will increase the subunits' authority. Authority is important to a subunit because it will specifically detail the amount of control it has within the organization. The more authority the subunit is able to acquire, the more influence it will achieve in the decision-making process. Third, subunits will be able to increase their control over resources. Fourth, the design of the organization's structure and culture can increase the control of information for subunits. The control of information will enable the subunits to have access to information in order to make better decisions that are in line with the strategic vision of the company.

Next, subunits will gain more centrality based on the design of the organization's structure and culture. Centrality allows subunits to control the information that is needed in order to reduce the level of risk and uncertainty needed during the decision-making process. With an increase in centrality, the level of uncertainty within subunits will decrease. This situation will lead to improved decision-making and an improved competitive advantage for the organization.

The culture and structure of the organization determine the power of the subunits by controlling their access to knowledge and resources. The structure and culture controls what information the different subunits will receive and the amount of influence they have in the organization. The culture and structure of an organization will increase the centrality of the subunits. Centrality is important to allow the subunits to accept their duties and responsibilities in order to continue to enhance their reputations and worth in the organization. Finally, a subunit is only influential if it is able to produce added value, which can only occur when it is an integral piece in the hierarchy and culture.

Values are determined by the customs and beliefs of a specific culture and its voice. The values of a culture include the principles of honesty, ethics, loyalty and responsibility. When entering into a new market segment in a foreign country, companies must learn and understand the various beliefs and values of both the consumers and employees. Since values will determine an individual's work ethic and preferences, companies will need to develop a reward system that gains the loyalty and support of both the employees and consumers. For consumers, companies will want to offer products that do not offend or undermine the existing values of the culture.

Attitudes are a representation of the fundamental values of a culture. Next, attitudes are based on individual feelings about the customs and traditions of a culture. The actions or behavior of an individual will be determined by their personal thoughts or beliefs. Finally, attitudes will express an individual's willingness to accept or reject a specific belief or orientation to a predefined value within the culture.

Values and attitudes are similar. First, values and attitudes are learned from the other members in the community. Parents, teachers and religious leaders that have served as important members in the community will help to spread their beliefs to future generations. Next, values and attitudes are based on the same core components. They both share a similar cognitive component or belief in the culture. Second, values and attitudes provoke an emotional feeling or reaction within the culture. Finally, both values and attitudes provide an individual with an intended reaction or feelings about someone or something.

However, values and attitudes are also different. When competing in international markets, firms must incorporate the different beliefs and values of the consumers and employees in the market segment. Since values will determine an individual's work ethic and preferences, companies will need to develop a reward system that gains the loyalty and support of both the employees and the consumers. Failure to offer a reward system will cause the company to disrespect the values and attitudes of the culture.

First, people in various cultures will have different attitudes about time. Depending on the country, attitudes about time can be flexible in order to allow employees and consumers the ability to enjoy their time. However, attitudes about time can also focus on effectiveness and efficiency. Deadlines must be followed and timelines met. Corporations will need to understand the cultural expectation in regard to time so the market segment is not offended by the business practices or values of the firm causing disconnects between the attitudes and values of the culture.

Second, people in different cultures will have various opinions about work. In some cultures, there is a strong work ethic and people live to work while other cultures believe that work is only done in order to live and to provide the resources for a happy life. When conducting business in a foreign culture, the firm must understand the different attitudes about work and to set up a corporate structure that accommodate the culture. The religion, education and personal communication skills of each culture must be identified in order to avoid offending the population and to provide high-quality outputs to meet the needs of the consumers that satisfied the current attitudes and values of the culture.

Finally, the manners and customs of people must be understood and not just assumed. The manners and customs of a culture will impact the physical environment when conducting businesses or negotiating a sale with the foreign market. If a company fails to understand the values and attitudes of the people, the firm would be viewed as trying to change the values and attitudes of the nation. This situation can lead to cultural diffusion and allow cultures to spread into new territories or cultural imperialism which would cause an existing culture to be replaced by a new culture.

Shared leadership and the valuing of voice has evolved from when it was first introduced over two decades ago. The idea of accessing the collective wisdom of stakeholders within an organization seemed misguided and frivolous. Wasting time with getting stakeholders to share their understanding and perceptions of how to address issues within an organization seemed like it was an endeavor of little or no returns. What we all have learned is that shared leadership does work. The idea of sharing the many roles and responsibilities of leadership with engaged stakeholders allows for each member to assume some of the burden of expectation of the team. Leaders believed that because of their position and access to information they were the best choice to make organizational decisions and to set the path for future operational systems. Many leaders saw shared leadership as a threat to their authority and their work as leaders. However, over time leaders recognized that if they wanted to make the best decisions possible, they needed to embrace that they do not know every answer. In many cases, they may not even know every question. It is the role of leaders to engage, activate and embrace the stakeholders around them to help move the organization forward.

The continued evolution that has been addressed within this text is that shared leadership alone is not sufficient in continuing to move organizations forward into continuous improvement. For example, schools must continuously seek ways to better engage and energize students so that they have access to complex and enlightened learning that is meaningful and valuable. Schools are continuously in search of the best way to connect with students and have them access their academic strengths so that they can meet with as much academic success as possible.

How can schools or any organization embrace continuous improvement and embrace the process of change to better meet its goals and expectations? If we all can agree that shared leadership works, but there is something else that needs to be done to ensure success that would be valuing voice. The process of honoring and respecting the diverse perspectives and experiences of each stakeholder. The belief that each stakeholder has spent time and energy working in the organization and has gathered a unique historical lens of what they have witnessed and experienced. If the organization or the school believes that it can improve and wants to engage in the process of change, then it has to determine how it will create a supportive system that respects each stakeholder and has a system that welcomes the leadership and sharing of all members of the team.

Now that the team of stakeholders has an ingrained belief that the valuing of voice is the keystone to their foundation of their work, they can then access the skills and interactions of shared leadership. Traditionally, the working theory is that shared leadership is the foundation of a system of embracing and collaborating as members of the organization. What we have argued and demonstrated is that prior to opening leadership and sharing the roles and responsibilities of leadership, an organization has to first embrace the value of voice of all stakeholders both internal and external stakeholders.

To truly honor the value of voice the stakeholders must create an environment that welcomes and respects the dissenting voice. The dissenting voice may have several characteristics that drive resistance. There could be a genuine fear of change. That change could cause a loss of power or influence that stakeholders do not welcome as part of their future organizational interactions. Or the dissenting stakeholder feels that their environment will change, and they will not understand expectations and/or outcomes. Or the dissenting voice might realize that if change happens that their role could be eliminated and their job will be different.

By valuing voice, the leader and other stakeholders can embrace the dissenting voice and use much of their perspective to help address fears and gaps in the operating system. The team can use the dissenting voice to help determine flaws in the action plans and reaching the established goals. The value of voice also will reduce the resistance of the dissenting voice because they were part of the process of change. They were members of the team that recommended the changes. This is significant because as the organization or school moves to implement, the team does not want conflicting messaging caused by the disconnected dissenting voice. By engaging all stakeholders in the valuing of voice, the organization make clear that it values all members and that their beliefs and perspectives are important.

Through our examination of shared leadership, we recognized that there is a need to explain how the value of voice should operate simultaneously and, in many ways, drive interactions and discussions. The value of voice is not something that only certain organizations can accomplish or that the organization must be a certain size. The leadership and the stakeholders must believe that there is a need for change and that process includes the value of voice. Through open exchanges among the stakeholders, the organization can access shared leadership and valuing of voice.

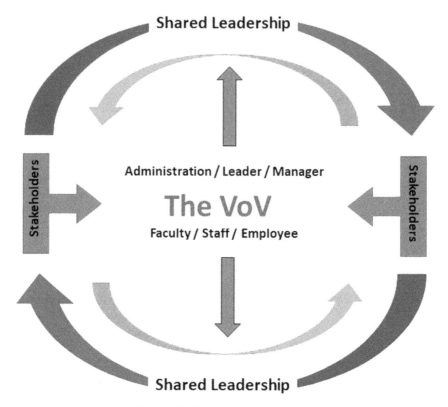

**Figure 12** The value of voice (VoV).

# EPILOGUE: ABACUS TO ANALYTICS AND STRATEGIES IN LEADERSHIP, MANAGEMENT AND THE VALUE OF VOICE

When I was younger, I loved playing games. The abacus, the first counting tool ever invented, could be bought and sold at local toy stores. I slid the colored beads back and forth the oblong rows as it taught me how to count. The game Monopoly could also be found in the toy department. It was my favorite game. I only had one rule when I played, and that was to be the banker. Oddly enough when I was the banker, I won. I must admit I would have made Don Corleone proud with the way I hid money and "cooked the books" against my fellow players. I believed that whoever controlled the money had the best strategy to win. In the beginning, this worked and I was undefeated. But like any criminal mastermind who tries to cheat at Monopoly, someone comes along with a better strategy. This strategy was simply called business analytics and that is the new strategy accounting and management need today.

I used to think that business was about "me" and what I could get out of it. I did not take into account the importance of voice, even when it came down to the numbers. Accounting is based on the standard and principle of numbers, which is the universal language of all business. Accountants would track the money to produce balance sheets, income statements, statements of cash flows, profit and loss statements and tax analysis. These documents were crucial to giving the manager an overview of where the business stood financially at any given point in time. It helps to keep businesses socially responsible. Accounting is necessary for a business to ensure that the financial information is recorded accurately based on the Securities and Exchange Commission. Socially responsible companies need to ethically and accurately report the revenue and losses to provide investors with the correct information.

However, the information produced with the traditional accounting standards were based on past data. With just this data alone, businesses are unequipped to deal with crisis management that will undoubtedly occur in an ever-changing global economy. A crisis is an event that will dramatically affect the operational process and strategy of an organization. In today's global economy, there is an increased probability of a complex disasters and emergencies. Crisis management is needed to study the data and analyze the potential for weaknesses and threats to the business and its stakeholders. Market segments in the global economy are sporadic and hard to predict due to the different variables that can affect the level of supply and demand. In order to prepare for disasters and potential emergencies, a company would need to have the ability to make critical decisions in a short amount of time. This situation would help to reduce or eliminate the level of risk or uncertainty to avoid a crisis. While accounting provides the foundation for making a decision, it then needs to be combined with another business principle which is business analytics.

Business analytics is a financial and data management solution that helps all businesses make smarter and better-informed decisions based on data mining, date aggregation and predictive methodologies. With business analytics, the information provided by doing accounting is combined with management strategies to determine the best possible outcome. This is just as important for small businesses, which make up more than 70 percent of the business market but have a 90 percent failure rate within the first five years as it is to companies that operate in industries that include health care, education, contracting, retail and energy.

So how do businesses need to develop a strategy of accounting management? There are several different things that businesses need to do to create an accounting and management strategy. First, businesses need to develop and implement a strategy that is action-oriented and is driven by business operations. Businesses will need to make sure that the strategy-execution process is implemented by the managers so they can determine what the company must do differently in order to improve the overall quality of production. Second, business company executives would need to develop a team effort among the employees. It is critical that every employee becomes an active participant in the strategy-execution process. Employees must be able to visualize the strategy in order to become part of the organization's team. This is done by transparency and sharing the necessary data, so it becomes more relevant to each employee. When the employee has a "what's in it for me" mentality, they are more willing to becoming involved in the team effort. As a result, the strategy-execution process will be implemented and carried out to completion.

Next, combining accounting principles with business analytics will help the business to properly utilize and allocate all of its resources. Businesses will want to make sure that managers and every department have an accurate budget in order to execute the strategy. Fourth, supportive policies and procedures would need to be established. Employees are resistant to change.

Executives will want to remove any obstacles of resistance to change in order to proceed with the execution of strategy. Failure to eliminate this obstacle will cause the strategy to not be implemented.

Fifth, businesses must adopt processes for continuous improvement. Six Sigma and establishing a high benchmark for quality control will ensure the success of strategy implementation. Integration is required to increase the efficiency of the company's core competencies and business model. Sixth, business analytics will revolutionize the culture of the business. Culture is important in becoming an ally to the execution of the business' strategy. Corporate culture helps to bring every employee together as a cohesive unit.

In order for businesses to lead with business analytics, it is important to use and build upon the core capabilities of the business. The development of a strong internal value chain will help the business to execute the desired strategy. Businesses also need to recognize that employees are the main resource for the company and should use them to help with new innovation and business processes. With the change from relying on either accounting or management, the combination of both will lead to smarter decisions and a more secure placement in the market based on the combination of methodologies with analytics. The change begins with a new focus from understanding the why and applying it to the how.

Finally, with the change from an abacus to business analytics mentality, your business will develop a balanced scorecard. A balanced scorecard is a performance measurement system that combines a "balance" between both financial and strategic objectives. The balanced scorecard is used by businesses to help balance out the overall goals of the organization by analyzing them strategically and financially. The balanced scorecard allows an organization to show the relationship between a strategic action and the financial impact it has on the entire organization so performance can be measured. It also helps to show a strong correlation between job functions and the impact they have on the organization's results. The balanced scorecard is a necessary tool in accurately and fairly evaluating an organization's performance that can only be done with business analytics.

With these skills, it is time to reinvent your business strategy remembering the importance of numbers, but more importantly understanding how they should be applied for future business decisions with respect to voice. Everything a business does gives value to voice. With business analytics, businesses everywhere can eliminate the fear of the five-year failure mark. Instead, they can flourish and expand into new niche markets. Now it is time to get out the old Monopoly board. Since I am no longer allowed to be the banker (and for good reason), I must use business analytics to win and make my opponents and "voice" offer they cannot refuse.

# INDEX

Page numbers in **bold** indicate figures and tables in the text.

Lightning Source UK Ltd.
Milton Keynes UK
UKHW010848231122
412665UK00003B/71